TEEN SUICIDE

TEEN SUICIDE

TEEN SUICIDE
The Raw Truth

Tracey Mullins

TEEN SUICIDE
THE RAW TRUTH

iUniverse books may be ordered through booksellers or by contacting:

iUniverse
1663 Liberty Drive
Bloomington, IN 47403
www.iuniverse.com
1-800-Authors (1-800-288-4677)

ISBN: 978-1-5320-8654-0 (sc)
ISBN: 978-1-5320-8653-3 (e)

Library of Congress Control Number: 2019917444

Print information available on the last page.

iUniverse rev. date: 11/12/2019

CONTENTS

CONTENTS

This book is dedicated to all the children who think there is no other answer but to end your life. You have so much to live for and you may feel like no one likes, loves or wants you but I can assure you there are people who do.

"Hold it all together everybody needs you strong, but life hits you out of nowhere and barely leaves you holding on. So, when you're on your knees and answers seem so far away, you're not alone, stop holding on and just be held. Your worlds not falling apart, it's falling into place I'm on the throne, stop holding on and just be held".

Casting Crowns

PREFACE

When you see the words *teen suicide*, what goes through your mind? Today, suicide is in too many conversations and being seen on the news daily. It is hard enough to grasp adults committing suicide, but being forced to grasp children killing themselves is just unthinkable. Unfortunately, today, suicide is becoming an answer for our children. "Every forty seconds there is an individual eighteen and under who has no other answer but to kill themselves."[1] This leads to the deaths of approximately eight hundred thousand children each year by suicide. These numbers do not include the attempts of suicide by individuals who were not successful. "Suicide is the second highest cause of death." Surely, I am not the only one that sees a serious problem with this information.[2]

Suicide typically happens in a moment of an individual's crisis, and the definition of crisis for a child can be different than the definition for an adult. Crises for children include the breakup from a partner, abuse from others, discrimination, or teasing and bullying by peers or family. It is important to note that it is not just one crisis that has happened to your child; it is crisis after crisis. Children today are more outspoken and often express themselves without caring who they may harm by using hurtful words. Not only do children have to hear remarks from peers

---

[1] Sarah Boseley, "Suicide kills one person worldwide every 40 seconds, WHO report finds," (September 4, 2014): Retrieved July 7, 2018, from https://www.theguardian.com/society/2014/sep/04/suicide-kills-every-40-seconds-who

[2] Ibid

at school, but social media is a harsh target as well. I will talk about social media and the damage it does to our children later in the book.

I have my MBA in psychology and am finishing my PhD in clinical psychology. I have talked with children who are harming themselves and want to kill themselves. I am writing this book to grab the attention of teens, parents, schools, and even bullies around the world. This book is the raw truth and must be spoken to take a step forward to save the hurting youth and teens who may feel they are better off dead. Some may feel the raw truth should not be spoken. Today it is the rawness that could lead parents, teachers, and peers to ask for help if needed and take the leading role of opening their eyes and ears, which, in return, would start saving lives. If you see fault in yourself, remember that it is never too late to change and become aware of everyone around you. Our children need us, and we must not forget how much they really need us.

I ask every reader to read with an open mind, and if my writing makes you angry or pissed off, let me apologize. My intensions here are good, and I hope to see parents, teachers, and our children make a change in their lives—a change of standing up and wanting to help those who are in need.

Readers will read and learn the following:
- suicide statistics
- myths about suicide
- what you don't know about today's teens
- top reasons for suicide
- what teens are saying
- what parents must do for early detection and prevention
- what happens after suicide is attempted
- a list of books for parents, teachers, and children, along with online resources that will help anyone in need

Throughout the book one will find short paragraphs about a child who took his or her own life. Unfortunately, they are real, and reading them may be shocking, but I do feel shock is what we need right now for a serious matter. I am hoping that somehow it will help others who feel alone or are contemplating taking their lives to talk to someone and receive the help they truly need. Bless these children and their families.

For those who are contemplating suicide, if you see this book, know that life is hard, but nothing is worth taking your own life. You must believe and have faith that your thoughts and situations will change. You cannot be afraid to reach out and ask for help. Feelings of depression and anxiety, being bullied, or enduring sexual abuse are big topics for you to handle alone. Whatever is affecting you, you are not alone. There is help out there, and you must reach out. Do not let anything or anyone determine when it is time for you to leave. You are in control of *your* life. Many of us adults have felt the pain you are going through right now, and there are many children feeling exactly what you feel right now. Although you may feel alone, you are not alone. I plea that if you are reading this and you have feelings of suicide, please talk to someone and ask for help. You have bigger plans in your future. Do not let someone take that away from you.

ACKNOWLEDGMENTS

I would like to start by thanking Sarah, my Realtor who became a dear friend. Who would have thought having lunch with you would turn into you inspiring me to write my heartfelt thoughts and my deepest feelings and passion on suicide. I cannot thank you enough for your encouragement, and I hope I have done you proud!

I would like to thank the children who let me interview them and trusting me with their words. All of you are very strong individuals, and it is a pleasure watching you all grow and overcome what life throws at you.

I would like to thank Kayla, my photographer who is also a dear friend. Thank you for the time you gave me and getting the right shot! It was hot and we were up against a lot of mosquitoes, but you are a professional and I love the end result.

Brent Burich, thank you for my cover design. I have always been a fan of your work. I would also like to thank your daughter Katarina Bennett for posing such a hard and emotional pose.

A huge thank you to everyone on my editorial team. I appreciate all the advice and the understanding of how important this book is to me. I know without this team my book would still be a draft somewhere in my computer. Thank you for bringing it alive!

I would like to thank Jaime Long, who I believe is my biggest fan! Jaime, you are always there to push me, encourage me, and help me believe in myself. Thank you for letting me bounce ideas your way, and thank you for your honesty! You are always so positive, and I cannot express how much your friendship means to me. I love you, and thank you so very much!

Mom, I love you! Thank you for showing your excitement of my book, for staying up late and reading it, and for encouraging me as you always have and do. Thank you for being my mother and friend!

Lois, my mother-in-law who is like my mother, you are always expressing how proud you are of me, and I hold your words very close to my heart. I love you, and I thank you for your advice and your stories you give to me.

To my husband, Mark; my daughters, Alexx and Madison; my son, Marcus; and my stepdaughter, Brook: saying I love you does not seem to be enough. Mark, you are my husband, my best friend, and my rock. You have sat back and let me run after my dreams. Because of you, I finished my MBA, began my PhD, completed my book, and started my own business. You share my smiles, laughter, and tears. You are my world, and my world would be nothing without you and our children. I love you with all my heart and soul. My children, I am so proud of all you, and I love you very much. Don't ever give up; keep chasing until you catch what you're dreaming of. It will happen. It takes God, family, friends, and patience!

A tragic loss that should not have happened ... Rest in peace, Katelyn.

Katelyn (2004–2016), age twelve, killed herself by hanging herself from a tree in her front yard. She committed her suicide while livestreaming. About a month prior to her suicide, she made several videos. Katelyn suffered from depression and was bullied at school. Katelyn claimed her father neglected her, and her stepfather physically and sexually abused her.[3]

A tragic loss that should not have happened ... Rest in peace, Audrie.

Audrie (1997–2012), age fifteen, a student attending high school in California died of suicide by hanging. She had allegedly been sexually assaulted by three teenage boys at a party. Eight days prior to her suicide pictures of the assault were posted online, and she was then being bullied because of the pictures.[4]

A tragic loss that should not have happened ... Rest in peace, Amanda.

Amanda (1996–2012), age fifteen, was a high school student who died of suicide by hanging herself because of students bullying and cyberbullying her. Prior to her suicide, Amanda posted a video on YouTube. She used flash cards to express her experience of being blackmailed by exposing her breasts on a webcam. Amanda also expressed about how she was bullied and physically assaulted.[5]

---

[3] "List of Suicides That Have Been Attributed to Bullying." (2018): Retrieved July 7, 2018, from https://infogalactic.com/info/List_of_suicides_which_have_been_attributed_to_bullying

[4] "3 U.S. teens arrested for sexual battery after girl's suicide," CBC News. (April 12, 2013): Retrieved July 7, 2018, from http://www.cbc.ca/news/canada/nova-scotia/story/2013/04/12/ns-rehteah-audrey-alleged-bullying-sex-assault.html

[5] "Amanda Todd Tribute Honors Life of Bullied Teen," News. Calgary, CA: CBC. (November 18, 2012): Retrieved July 7, 2018, from https://www.cbc.ca/news/canada/british-columbia/amanda-todd-tribute-honours-life-of-bullied-teen-1.1138838

CHAPTER 1

The Raw Truth

According to the National Conference of State Legislatures (NCSL, 2018), 19.3 percent of high school students have seriously considered killing themselves, 14.5 percent of high school students made actual plans for committing suicide, and 900,000 youth and teens have planned their suicides during an episode of major depression.[6]

The National Conference of State Legislatures also shares that suicide is the fourth leading cause of death for young people between the ages of ten and fourteen. Females are prone to contemplate suicide twice as much as a male, but males are four times more likely to follow through with suicide.[7]

According to Teen Suicide Statistics, females who commit suicide will likely choose death by overdosing on pills or cutting themselves. Males tend to use a lethal and quick way to commit suicide. Males will use a gun, jump from a high place, or hang themselves. This is one of the reasons males succeed in their suicide attempts. While doing some of

---

[6] Teen Suicide Statistics (2018) Teen Suicide Facts. Retrieved July 7, 2018 from http://teensuicidestatistics.com/statistics-facts.html

[7] Ibid.

research, I noticed that girls are starting to hang themselves just as often as boys. I am sure in the future some of these statistics will change.[8]

The National Conference of State Legislatures (NCSL) reports suicide for those age twenty-four and younger has increased by 6 percent. However, suicide for ages ten to fourteen has increased by 100 percent. According to the American Foundation for Suicide Prevention in Texas, the number of deaths by suicide in 2017 was 3,403. Suicide is the eleventh leading cause of death in Texas. On an average, one person dies by suicide every three hours in Texas.[9]

A tragic loss that should not have happened … Rest in peace, Coby.

Coby (2005–2018), age twelve, was a high school student who was bullied at school and was afraid to go to school. His mother knew this was going on because he would come home crying daily. His mother expressed to him he had to go to school. He was ready to go to school, and while his mother was on the phone with his father, he went to his room and shot himself in the head. He did this with his mother's gun, which had been in a safe. He did not want to go to school because he could not bear another day of the bullying.[10]

A tragic loss that should not have happened … Rest in peace, Jadin.

Jadin (1997–2013) became known for his suicide, which raised the national profile on youth bullying and gay victimization in bullying. Jadin was a fifteen-year-old gay youth who was allegedly intensely bullied both in person and cyberbullied because he was gay. Jadin hung

---

[8] Ibid.

[9] Ibid.

[10] "List of Suicides That Have Been Attributed to Bullying." (2018): Retrieved July 7, 2018, from https://infogalactic.com/info/List_of_suicides_which_have_been_attributed_to_bullying

himself from a play structure at an elementary school. He did not die right away, but after being taken off of life support, he passed away.[11]

A tragic loss that should not have happened … Rest in peace, Jamey.

Jamey (1997–2011), age fourteen, was a gay teenager and was an activist against homophobia. He made videos trying to help and put a stop to homophobic bullying. He ended his life by hanging himself, because of the constant bullying.[12]

Additional facts about suicide in the United States include the following:
- The annual age-adjusted suicide rate is 13.42 per 100,000 individuals.[13]
- On average, there are 123 suicides per day.[14]
- Firearms accounted for 51 percent of all suicides in 2016.[15]
- Males die by suicide 3.53 times more often than females.[16]
- For every suicide, there are twenty-five attempts that were not successful.[17]
- Suicide costs the United States $69 billion annually.[18]

---

[11] Associated Press. "Jadin Bell Dead: Gay Oregon Teen Who Hanged Himself Dies After Being Taken Off Life Support," *Huffington Post* (February 4, 2013): Retrieved July 7, 2018, from https://www.huffpost.com/entry/jadin-bell-dead-gay-oregon-teen hanging_n_2617909

[12] Howlett, Karen. "Anti-bullying Bill Passes, Clearing Way for Gay-Straight Alliances in Ontario Schools." *The Globe and Mail* (June 5, 2012): Accessed July 7, 2018. https://www.theglobeandmail.com/news/politics/anti-bullying-bill-passes-clearing-way-for-gay straight-alliances-in-ontario-schools/article4231542/.

[13] Teen Suicide Statistics (2018): Teen Suicide Facts. Retrieved July 7, 2018 from http://teensuicidestatistics.com/statistics-facts.html

[14] Ibid.

[15] Ibid.

[16] Ibid.

[17] Ibid.

[18] Ibid.

When looking at facts like these, my hope is that it is affecting you as it has me. So many young children are taking their lives because they feel unwanted or are suffering from a mental illness and they feel there is no reason to be a part of this society. Can you imagine a five-year-old feeling there is no hope for him and hanging himself to let his parents find him? It is difficult to delve into why a child may try to commit suicide or what it would be like for the parents of that child to find them. It is natural to wonder who is to blame in such circumstances.

Our children should not feel like there is no reason to live, feel like nobody loves them, feel like nobody would care, or feel like nobody cares that people are bullying them. They should not ask themselves the question, "Why am I even here?" We must step up and change the way these children are thinking and feeling.

These children are begging for help prior to their suicides. Why are we not seeing the signs, why are we not believing them, and why do we care after the act to find signs prior to the suicide? The caring is needed before children feel the loneliness that will push them to end it all.

Questions about what is happening to a child who wants to kill herself should be asked, especially if one is a parent or schoolteacher. The people who commit suicide are all around you. Later in the book you will find information to help you identify a child or person in need of help. But first, we'll look at some myths surrounding suicide.

CHAPTER 2

Myths about Suicide

Myths stand in the way of helping understand your child's true needs. We must address the myths, so we can educate others on suicide and the real, raw facts.

Myth: People feel if they approach their children about suicide it will encourage them to make suicide attempts. *Wrong!*[19]

When talking to your child about suicidal thoughts, it will open the doors for communication between you and your child. If your child hears you speak of the reasons to live, it will encourage her to live. Encourage your child, and do not be afraid to talk to them about any thoughts or situations.

Myth: Children only talk about killing themselves. They won't really do it. *Wrong!*[20]

If your child talks about killing himself, it is his last request for help. If your child is talking, he has started planning. Talk to your child, ask if he is thinking about killing himself and ask him if he already has a

---

[19] Office of Suicide Prevention. "The Myths & Facts of Youth Suicide," (2019): Retrieved July 7, 2018, from suicideprevention.NV.gov/Youth/Myths/

[20] Ibid

plan put into place. Talk to your child, and put a personal safety plan in use. Seek help immediately.

Myth: An attempt or a successful suicide comes without warning. *Wrong!*[21]

Children who survived their attempts of suicide admit there were signs for people. They just did not realize it or ignored them.

Myth: A child who attempted suicide but survived will never attempt suicide again. *Wrong!*[22]

When your child attempts suicide and survives, she will attempt again but will add more danger to the suicide attempt, meaning she will change how she did it the first time.

A tragic loss that should not have happened … Rest in peace.

> One pill Two pills Three Pills Four …
> Just a little more …
> Five pills Six pills Seven pills Eight …
> Can't help me now …
> It's too late … [23]

A tragic loss that should not have happened … Rest in peace.

> Dead …
> He killed me …
> Bullied …
> No more pain …
> 13 years of age … [24]

Myth: Once a child decides to kill himself, there is no changing his mind. *Wrong!*[25]

---

[21] Ibid

[22] Ibid

[23] Bing (2018): Sad Suicide Notes. Retrieved July 7, 2018, from http:///bing.com

[24] Ibid

[25] Office of Suicide Prevention. "The Myths & Facts of Youth Suicide," (2019): Retrieved July 7, 2018, from suicideprevention.NV.gov/Youth/Myths/

Suicides can be stopped at any time. Your child can be helped. Do not ever just give into the situation. A crisis is short-lived; suicide is forever.

Myth: A child only cries suicide to get attention. *Wrong!*[26]

You cannot just dismiss a suicide threat because you think your child is wanting attention. Truth be said, you already missed the cry for help a long time ago. Do not make the last mistake and brush it off thinking your child just wants attention.

Myth: Suicide is hereditary. *Wrong!*[27]

It is possible to see several members in a family commit suicide, but it is not because it is hereditary. The harsh truth is they all live in the same emotional environment; therefore, one suicide will raise the thought of suicide as if that is the only answer to end the pain they are going through.

Myth: Only certain types of people will kill themselves. *Wrong!*[28]

This makes me angry. What does that mean, *certain types*? Every one of us has the risk of suicide. Predisposing conditions can lead anyone to attempt or complete their suicide. These conditions can include depression, mental disorder, substance abuse, or being emotional. Every person is in danger of committing suicide.

A tragic loss that should not have happened ... Rest in peace, Rebecca.

Rebecca (2000–2013), age twelve, was a middle school student who committed suicide by jumping off a tower due to bullying. Rebecca was cyberbullied and bullied in person for a year and a half. Two girls, ages fourteen and twelve, encouraged peers to fight Rebecca. They would also send messages telling her to kill herself. Her mother said she would come home in tears almost every day.[29]

---

[26] Ibid.

[27] Ibid

[28] Ibid

[29] "Rebecca Sedwick Case: Bullied Girl and Her Tormentor Both Grew Up in 'disturbing' family situations, says sheriff," Retrieved July 7, 2018, from https://www.nydailynews.com/news/national/rebecca-sedwick-case-suicide-victim-bully-grew-disturbing-family-homes-article-1.1496991

A tragic loss that should not have happened … Rest in peace, Tyler.

Tyler (1992–2009), age seventeen, was a homosexual student with Asperger's syndrome. Students would steal from him, spit in his food, and call him names such as "gay" and "faggot." His mother went to the school, and all the school said was, "Boys will be boys." Wearing his favorite T-shirt and jeans, Tyler took his life by hanging himself in his closet.[30]

A tragic loss that should not have happened … Rest in peace, Phoebe.

Phoebe (1994–2010), age fifteen, was a high school student who died by hanging herself because of school bullying and cyberbullying. There were six students who were charged for the bullying. Their sentence after their guilty pleas was community service and probation.[31]

Myth: There is no need to worry about your child who attempted suicide. *Wrong!*[32]

Three months after your child's first attempt is a dangerous time. When she seems to be feeling better or acting like life is great, it is because she has made another plan—a plan that will complete the attempt.

Myth: If your child is suicidal, he will always be suicidal. *Wrong!*[33]

If you take the action seriously, your child will receive the help he needs, and he can live through this hard time and live a healthy life, which will be free from suicidal thoughts.

---

[30] "Bullied to Death in America's Schools-ABC News," Retrieved July 7, 2018, from https://abcnews.go.com/2020/TheLaw/school-bullying-epidemic-turning-deadly/story?id=11880841

[31] "Grand Jury Indicts 9 Students in Connection with Phoebe Prince Bullying Case," Gazettenet.com. Retrieved July 7, 2018, from http://www.cnn.com/2010/CRIME/03/29/massachusetts.bullying.suicide/index.html

[32] Office of Suicide Prevention. "The Myths & Facts of Youth Suicide," (2019): Retrieved July 7, 2018, from suicideprevention.NV.gov/Youth/Myths/

[33] Ibid

Myth: Children typically resent others who try to change their minds on suicide. *Wrong!*[34]

It is common for a child to become angry or defensive, but it is her way of protecting her decision. Once the walls are broken, the child appreciates the people who cared for her and helped her overcome this time in her life.

Myth: A child will not really kill himself over a breakup. *Wrong!*[35]

A child may kill himself when losing someone he loves. He may not be able to handle the fact that the relationship failed.

Myth: Children who kill themselves were crazy and insane. *Wrong!*[36]

Yes, children do kill themselves because of depression, but this does not mean they are crazy or insane. Truth be said, there are some who do meet the criteria for mental illness, and they do need psychiatric help. However, this does not make them crazy or insane.

Myth: Most children who commit suicide do so in the cold winter months. *Wrong!*[37]

Most of our children will commit suicide in spring or early summer.

Myth: Every suicide is preventable. *Wrong!*[38]

There are times when a child has received top help, parents were by her side, and interventions were held, but the child continued her plan and unfortunately completed that plan. The main problem here is we all lack education in suicide.

We truly need to change our thought process. Anything is possible even when we feel it is not possible. If you think it can't or it won't, you are *wrong* because it can and it will! The next chapter will look at what types of problems teens face.

---

[34] Ibid

[35] Ibid

[36] Ibid

[37] Ibid

[38] Office of Suicide Prevention. "The Myths & Facts of Youth Suicide," (2019): Retrieved July 7, 2018, from suicideprevention.NV.gov/Youth/Myths/

CHAPTER 3

Did You Know

People are often afraid to ask whether there is a problem, and as a result, our teens face deeply troubling issues alone.

Parents have no clue what is going on with their children most of the time. Parents may say, "He never said anything about depression," "She never told me others were bullying her at school," or "He never told me he did not fit in anywhere." As parents we should know our children inside and out. Parents should know if a child seems distant is showing signs of depression, and a child contemplating suicide always gives signs beforehand. We talk more about this in chapter 6, "What a Parent Must Do."

It's common to think that kids today have it easy, especially because they seem to have conveniences we did not have. But they do face complicated issues. Some of the issues our children face alone are teen suicide, cyberbullying, substance abuse, violence at home, and mental health problems. Some risk factors for teen suicide include a history of suicide attempts by a teen; family history of suicides; anxiety, depression, or drug abuse; and exposure to others committing suicide.

Our children have a lot of pressure on them, including what comes from parents, peers, coaches, and other family members. Their perspectives are often rooted in the now, so they are not able to see a future that's different. And if they are suffering, this can impact what they may think. That's why they need adults to help them.

Why is it so hard to sit down and talk with your children? Parents are so involved in their own needs and wants that they often forget to talk to their children. When I say this, I am referring to *real talk*. It should be a rule in every house that each night at dinner they sit as a family and talk. Ask questions about your children's day and their friends. A parent must ask questions to know what is going on in their children's lives. This is a big factor with people stepping in and speaking up or out about issues with teens. Most of the time people believe that if we ignore an issue, it will pass. We must stop sweeping things under the carpet. We must all stand up and start noticing what is going on in our own homes. Children need their parents, even when they say they don't, they do. They are starving for your attention.

You have more opportunities than you think to reach out to your children. Don't wait for a crisis. Talk to them at dinner, in the car, or even just in their rooms before going to bed at night. No matter how busy you are or how trivial their concerns may seem, making an effort to listen will show you care about what matters to them.

Next, we'll look at why children can feel that suicide is an answer.

CHAPTER 4

The Top Reasons for Teen Suicide

I mentioned earlier that one of the first questions people try to resolve when talking about a suicide is why. According to the Nemours Foundation, the reasons reported for a teen committing or attempting suicide are as follows:[39]

- mental disorders, including depression
- stress
- emotional neglect
- divorce
- domestic abuse
- sexual abuse
- drug and alcohol abuse
- sexual orientation
- peer pressure
- bullying and cyberbullying

---

[39] Nemours Foundation (1995–2019). "Why Do Teens Try to Kill Themselves?" Retrieved July 5, 2018, from https://kidshealth.org

I will take one reason at a time and explain each one in depth. It is important to know and understand what a child could be going through, which may eventually cause them to take his own life.

Mental Disorders

Mental illnesses affect how a person thinks. It is an illness, just as a physical illness is, and it often needs treatment by a doctor. There are many mental illnesses that affect both adults and children, and they include depression, suicidal thoughts, anxiety, obsessive-compulsive disorder (OCD), anorexia, and bulimia to name a few.

Studies show approximately 90 percent of teens who commit suicide have a diagnosable and treatable mental illness.[40] Sadly, less than half of these kids were diagnosed or treated for the mental disorder. Another sad fact is half of children who commit suicide will do so while under the influence of drugs or alcohol.[41] It is important to note that a sudden chronic illness or traumatic injury can lead to depression or psychological complications in children. It is also important to note that children who feel suicidal may mistake their thoughts for feeling depressed. According to the Nemours Foundation, "They're unaware that it is the depression. Not the situation, that's influencing them to see things in a 'there's no way out,' 'it will never get better,' 'there's nothing I can do' kind of way."[42]

If there is any family history with depression, drug or alcohol abuse, or suicides, your child is at a higher risk.

These mental illnesses can be misdiagnosed. This may be caused by parents not understanding the signs, which means there are signs not being reported to the doctor. This section will focus on depression.

---

[40] Teen Suicide Statistics (2018) Teen Suicide Facts. Retrieved July 7, 2018, from http://teensuicidestatistics.com/statistics-facts.html

[41] Ibid.

[42] Nemours Foundation. "Why Do Teens Try to Kill Themselves?" Retrieved July 5, 2018, from https://kidshealth.org

Depression. Feelings of depression are much like suicidal feelings, and it is important to know because depression is a huge silent killer. Depression is a persistent feeling of sadness or disconnect from the activates that once interested your teen. It affects how a person thinks, feels, and behaves and causes both emotional and physical problems.

Depression and suicidal feelings that accompany it are treatable mental disorders. The child needs to have the illness recognized by parents and diagnosed by a doctor. This will allow the doctor to apply the appropriate treatment plans for the child. Parents may not know if a child has a mental disorder; therefore, it is important to look for signs. When in doubt, a psychiatric assessment can be ordered from the child's doctor.

Parents should reach out to the child's doctor if they notice any of the following signs lasting for more than a week.

- changes in sleeping or eating behaviors or withdrawal from friends or family
- changes in personality or personal appearance, maybe even not participating in activities such as sports
- complaints of being sick all the time, such as always tired, frequent stomachaches, or recurring headaches
- unexpected anger or violent episodes
- the smell of any type of drugs or alcohol
- boredom or a struggle with concentrating on everyday tasks
- drawings or writing that focuses on death
- listens to music about death or sad feelings such as hopelessness
- falling grades in school
- frequent attempts to run away

These are good signs to watch. You should seek help if you notice any of these signs in your child.

As I have expressed, depression and suicide share many of the same signs. Take your teen's feelings seriously.

Suicidal Feelings: When a Child Is Ready to Act

The following signs are crucial. If you notice these signs, you need to seek help immediately.

- expression of feelings that things will not get better, feelings of helplessness to change situations, comments about dying or death, and threats of suicide even if they say they are kidding
- a child's belief that he is a bad child, feeling bad all the time, or thoughts about not being able to do well in anything
- the idea that death would mean he wouldn't be a problem for the family anymore (Some children will say things such as, "I will not be your problem anymore," "There is no use in living anymore," or, "I will not see you again." These statements are heart-wrenching.)
- the act of giving away possessions to family or friends; may even throw some important belongings away
- an unusually clean room or actions that appear to be a child putting his affairs in order
- becoming happy after having a severe episode of depression
- bizarre or puzzling thoughts

If you should ever hear your child or maybe your child's friend say she wants to kill herself or is contemplating suicide, be sure to take the comment seriously and get medical help from the child's doctor or a qualified mental health professional. One can always call 911 or the National Suicide Prevention Lifeline at 800-273-TALK (8255) or reach the Crisis Text Line by texting TALK to 741741.

Nobody likes to talk about death, but it is important to talk about death. It is okay to ask your child if he is depressed and contemplating suicide. Rest assured that you will not put the thought of suicide in his head if it is not what he is thinking. If a child is thinking about suicide, reaching out and asking will let him know you do care and you do pay attention. It will give the child an open door to talk to you. When there is support from family and treatment from a professional, children who think suicide is the only answer can begin to heal and get on the road to a healthy and successful life.

Stress

Stress comes from all around us. It affects all ages, and people may need to understand the term *all ages* a bit more. Our children go through a lot more stress than you may want to realize. Maybe to you, their stress is not bigger than your stress load, but let us not forget they are a lot younger than we are, and they do not fully understand how to deal with certain stress.

The following is a list of stressors that affect children:
- family stress
- peer/social pressure
- self-esteem, including bullying
- sexual stress, including sexual identity
- trauma/violence
- medical illness
- substance abuse
- grief and loss

Maybe you are a big part of the child's stress; for example, perhaps the pressure of getting good grades to become successful has become too much. Some parents feel their children should live up to certain standards, or they push their children because they do not want to be embarrassed if they are not in the top of the class, the captain of the football team, or head of the cheerleading squad. As an adult, how many times have you wanted everything to stop or go away? How can one expect a child to handle stress when sometimes we as adults cannot handle stress?

If you or anyone in your family has already had these issues, it is important you know that your child is affected by this. If you see any type of changes, seek the help that is necessary.

A tragic loss that should not have happened ... Rest in peace, Kenneth.

Kenneth (1997–2012), age fourteen, took his life by hanging himself in his garage. He was bullied, received death threats on his phone, and was the subject of a Facebook hate group for being gay. Kenneth expressed to his mom that she had no idea how it felt to be so hated.[43]

A tragic loss that should not have happened ... Rest in peace, Ty.

Ty (1998–2010), age eleven, was bullied for being too small for his age. Students would put him in lockers and trash cans. They called him names such as Tiny Tim and shrimp. Ty stood up for himself one day at school. He was pushed by one of his bullies, but this time Ty pushed back. After the two were sent to the office, Ty had to serve a three-day suspension and the bully only received a one-day suspension. After school that day, Ty committed suicide by shooting himself in the head with his father's .22 caliber pistol.[44]

A tragic loss that should not have happened ... Rest in peace, Jamie.

Jamie (1996–2011), age fifteen, was being bullied by students because she was gay. After Jamie's suicide, her parents announced a new federal antibullying strategy where teens hold workshops and give presentations in an effort to build awareness for students who are being bullied.[45]

---

[43] "Kenneth Weishuhn, Gay Iowa Teen, Commits Suicide after Allegedly Receiving Death Threats," *Huffington Post* (April 17, 2012): Retrieved July 7, 2018, from https://www.huffpost.com/entry/kenneth-weishuhn-gay-iowa-teen-suicide_n_1431442

[44] "A Father Fights Bullying," (May 14, 2010): Retrieved July 7, 2018, from www.greatschools.org/.../a-father-fights-bullying

[45] Howlett, Karen. "Anti-bullying Bill Passes, Clearing Way for Gay-Straight Alliances in Ontario Schools." *The Globe and Mail* (June 5, 2012): Accessed July 7, 2018. https://www.theglobeandmail.com/news/politics/anti-bullying-bill-passes-clearing-way-for-gay straight-alliances-in-ontario-schools/article4231542/.

Emotional Neglect

Typically, when people hear about neglect, they tend to believe it is from no food, an unsafe environment, or lack of proper clothing for the child. What people need to pay attention to is failing to provide emotional support to a child. Emotional support is just as import as food, clothing, and shelter. If you do not give the emotional needs to your child, such as emotional support or seeking a doctor's help if your child is showing signs of depression or behavioral problems, this is known as emotional neglect.

Today both parents are often working outside the home, and this is not a bad thing; however, it leads to the parents being very much involved in their area of work. Although this does not mean we do not care for our children, children tend to believe their parents do not care as much for them. Parents, I know this is not what we expect to do, but let's face it: life is busy, and our goals are to provide our families with all the necessities and more. We kind of forget about the here and now. To be honest, the children need the here and now. While parents run around trying to take care of the future, their children have too much freedom and start raising themselves. Is this what you had in mind when you decided to start a family? My answer is of course not, but it happens to all parents. Believe it or not, all of your future planning becomes emotional neglect to your children.

When parents give their children too much freedom or too many gifts instead of parenting, they will become undisciplined. This, in turn, leads to entitlement, which will eventually cause children to start feeling forgotten, alone, and without the care and love of others. Feelings such as these will lead to different thinking, such as no meaning to life or existence. All this leads children to underestimate their value to the family, friends, and themselves.

If children do not see they are making a difference in the lives of their parents, it will be impossible for the children to see they hold any significance with anyone, including their peers. The worst feeling any human being can experience is to feel he does not exist. Neglectful parents are shocked when a child attempts or commits suicide. These parents feel they gave the child everything they could financially and gave them freedom. The harsh lesson for a neglectful parent is that your children need and crave more than anything you buy them; it is your love and discipline they desire.

Parents can not realize the emotional neglect they have with their children, and others much be watchful. It is not hard to notice if parents behave in this manner, and it would be your responsibility to take action. How would you feel if you knew there was something wrong in a family concerning a child and you found out the child killed himself? Maybe if you would have told someone or sought out help for the child, he would still be alive. With that said, here are some important signs to watch for when around other parents and their children.

If you notice parents not spending time with their children, not showing affection, continually putting their children down, or never praising and encouraging the children, you may be witnessing emotional neglect.

Let me break this down, so you understand the meaning of these signs.

- *Ignoring of the child.* This is when the parent acts as if the child does not exist. It is known that parents who ignore their children were probably ignored as children. In return, the parent may not really understand the emotional needs of children and how important those needs are.
- *Corrupting the child.* This is when a parent allows the child to hurt others, use drugs, or watch inappropriate movies or otherwise exposes the child to situations that are not safe for the child.
- *Terrorizing the child.* The parent may attack the child or single a child out so the parent can punish or criticize that particular child.
- *Threatening to discipline in a severe way.* Setting their standards too high for the child to achieve allowing the child's negative self-worth to set in.

- *Isolating the child.* Parents who will not let their children join activities with peers or other family members. Parents who make their children stay in their rooms, keeping them locked up and tucked away.
- *Abusing the child verbally.* Verbal abuse is when a parent belittles the child, constantly threatening or ridiculing the child.
- *Denying the accusations.* If the parent is confronted by someone, he or she will deny and put blame on the child. This is a hard one because when parents are in denial or will not admit to doing things to their children, the children will stop telling others what is going on in the home due to the lack of evidence. As a result, the child will continue to take the emotional neglect.
- *Minimizing, which is less harsh than denying.* When a parent minimizes the accusations, it means the parent will not admit to the whole truth. The parent will start pointing the finger at the child and how the accusations are the child's fault. The truth of the matter is that it is the parent who has deep emotional problems.

It is important to add that emotional neglect or abuse is not partial to one type of parent. Emotional neglect happens in any environment, rich or poor, and any culture. However, it is important to reiterate that abusers were typically abused themselves while growing up. Other reasons for emotional neglect from a parent can be due to their stress and not having good parenting skills. These parents may not know about the resources that could help them be better parents. The abuser will be quick to say it is not their fault; they will make their children believe it is their fault and it is their actions that push the parents to act this way. Unfortunately, parents either do not comprehend or simply do not care how they are interfering with their children's cognitive development.

You may be asking yourself how you can tell if a child is being emotionally neglected. There are many signs to look for. For instance, you may notice a child who sucks or bites herself. The child may rock herself back and forth. The child may be very aggressive and destructive toward others. According to Teen Help (2018), Some children may have speech problems, demonstrate compulsive or obsessive behaviors, or show fears.[46] One may notice the child has nothing good to say about himself. The child may be very shy and suffer in areas such as physical, mental, or emotional development. The child can be harsh to others or very demanding.

Sadly, emotional neglect is hard to understand or comprehend by one who does not have these tendencies, specifically to the children who are going through this right now. These children suffer from psychological development and losing trust from an early age. These children cannot depend on the people who are supposed to be the ones who love them the most. When a child starts to distrust adults, it makes it extremely hard for someone outside to assist and offer help. Does this mean we stand back and watch it happen? No. It just means that, like any other problem, there is still hope, and one can step in and intervene to help. The impairment will not be overturned, but there is help available from professionals who can work with the child and the parents.

A tragic loss that should not have happened … Rest in peace, Kelly.

Kelly (1984–1997), age thirteen, committed suicide by overdose after she told her parents what she was going to do. She took her life because of bullying, taunting, and harassment because of her weight. On many occasions a group of kids between the ages of thirteen and seventeen would go to her home and throw food at her house while yelling cruel names. Kelly could not bear it anymore. Five kids were convicted of intentional harassment that led to a suicide.[47]

A tragic loss that should not have happened … Rest in peace, Hamed.

---

[46] TeenHelp.com, (2018): "Emotional Abuse." Retrieved July 1, 2018, from https://www.teenhelp.com

[47] "Bullied to Death in America's Schools-ABC News," Retrieved July 7, 2018, from https://abcnews.go.com/2020/TheLaw/school-bullying-epidemic-turning-deadly/story?id=11880841

Hamed (1985–2000), age fourteen, was a ninth grader who jumped from a bridge because of bullying. Hamed left his parents a note explaining students and even his friends were teasing him. They were calling him names such as big nose, geek, and four eyes. He could not take it anymore, so he put his new jacket on and went to the bridge where he ended his life.[48]

Divorce

Children have the tendency to personalize and think they are the cause of everything going wrong in the lives of loved ones. When parents divorce, their children may conclude they are the cause of the stress. They feel if they were good enough, their parents would work harder to stay together, or they feel if they were not there, their parents would stay together.

While there are some individuals who can go through a divorce without being immature, there are some divorcing parents who become self-centered and immature people. People who divorce are often cruel to each other. Their children become collateral, they try to alienate the kids from each other, and there is no stability. Kids need both their parents and even more so during a time of divorce.

One of the children I interviewed was in the midst of watching her parents go through a divorce. I was called in the middle of the night to come over and talk to this child. She began to cut herself. (This child was only twelve years of age at the time.) While sitting down with her and both parents, she began to talk to me about how she heard her mom and dad fight and could not handle it. She would actually rush in between them, telling them to stop. She expressed that maybe it would be better if she was not there, and I watched both parents drop their heads. I had asked if she really thought her parents would stay together if she was not there or not alive. Her answer was, "I don't know, but I would not have to hear them fight." What a sad answer from a child

---

[48] "School teasing blamed in Surrey teen's suicide" Archived from the original on May 12, 2001. Accessed July 7, 2018. https://www.cbc.ca/news/canada/school-teasing-blamed-in-surrey-teen-s-suicide-1.221495.

who wanted to see love from her parents. I would like to add that with her being brave and honest, I was able to work with the family and make the situation as smooth as it could be for the parents and their children.

Divorcing parents would hate to have their divorce and immature acting lead to a child committing suicide. Divorcing parents need to remember the divorce is to benefit all involved, especially and most importantly their children.

Sexual Abuse

There is often confusion over the phrase *sexual abuse* and what it entails. Sometimes people use this phrase to refer to rape, but there are different types of sexual abuse. Sexual abuse is when a child is coerced in some way to take part in a sexual activity. It can mean inappropriate touching or something more, but it doesn't always involve touching. Sometimes the child doesn't even know the act is wrong. However, a lot of times the child does, and living with the confusion and guilt can lead to suicide without the proper counseling.

Sexual assault is a specific type of sexual abuse, and it refers to sexual contact that occurs without explicit consent of the victim. Children who have been victims of sexual assault are at greater risk for suicide. "The stigma is often not addressed; it's a silent issue in society," says Laura Anderson, a licensed psychologist and assistant professor in the University at Buffalo School of Nursing. "Very rarely does programming address boys. It's often presumed to be an issue for girls. The results highlight the need to educate the public and develop preventive programming and support for male and female sexual assault survivors."[49]

Rape is a specific type of sexual assault, and it has a legal definition that varies from state to state. Being a rape victim myself, I cannot imagine a child being sexually assaulted, and it would be even worse to be assaulted by someone the child trusted. Children who are sexually

---

[49] Robinson-Buffalo. M. "Sexually Assaulted Teens at Greater Risk of Suicide." *Futurity*. Accessed. April 6, 2015 https://www.futurity.org/sexually-assault-boys-suicide-891742/.

abused are facing more than just the sexual part of the abuse. These children have completely lost trust, and they must live with this secret in fear. These children have been hurt, broken, and constantly injured. The abuser will program the child's mind. Abusers manipulate their victims, which is easy for them because their victims are children and children often believe what they have been told. Somehow, the abusers will make their victims feel as if the abuse is their fault.

Why are people so uncomfortable talking about this act? Why do parents or family members of the victim want to believe this is not true, the child has exaggerated, or the child just wants attention? How could anyone not believe or not want to help these poor victims? Personally, I believe these types of individuals should serve time in prison along with the abuser. To stand by and not do anything or to shut your eyes so you do not have to deal with this problem is just as bad as the sexual act that was done on the child.

Teen Dating Violence

Another type of sexual abuse is teen dating violence. Centers for Disease Control and Prevention define teen dating violence is physical, sexual, psychological, or emotional aggression in a dating relationship. This also includes a person who is stalking someone. This can happen in person or electronically. It can also happen in a current relationship or from a former partner.

This type of violence is happening everywhere. As with any other type of abuse, the effects are long term. Most teens will not report what is happening to them because they are afraid. It is said that 12 percent of high school females did report physical violence, and 16 percent reported sexual violence from the person she was dating. For males, 7 percent reported physical violence, and 5 percent reported sexual violence from the person he was dating.[50]

---

[50] "Preventing Intimate Partner Violence," Centers for Disease Control and Prevention. Retrieved July 7, 2018, from https://www.cdc.gov/violenceprevention/intimatepartnerviolence/fastfact.html

Centers for Disease Control found that among victims of contact sexual violence, physical violence, or stalking by intimate partner, 23 percent of females and 14 percent of males experienced some form of violence before the age of eighteen. Teens who are abused by a partner will suffer with long-term outcomes such as alcohol abuse, eating disorders, thoughts of suicide, and violent behaviors.[51]

A tragic loss that should not have happened … Rest in peace, Dawn-Marie.

Dawn-Marie (1986–2000), age fourteen, was a high school student who took her life by hanging herself with her dog's leash because of bullying. There were three females involved in her bullying. These three girls were both psychologically and verbally abusive. Dawn-Marie left a note to her parents explaining the torture she was going through. She felt she could not say anything because it would make it worse. She also felt if the girls were suspended from school, they would never leave her alone.[52]

A tragic loss that should not have happened … Rest in peace, Tyler.

Tyler (1991–2010), age eighteen, jumped to his death from the George Washington Bridge. His last words were posted onto his Facebook page prior to taking his life. "Jumping off the gw bridge sorry." Tyler's roommate used a webcam to view him kissing another man. The roommate then shared the view on Twitter while urging others to watch and pass it on. Tyler's death brought national and

---

[51] Ibid.

[52] "B.C. Girl Convicted in School Bullying Tragedy," CBC News (March 26, 2002): Retrieved July 7, 2018, from https://www.cbc.ca/news/canada/b-c-girl-convicted-in-school-bullying-tragedy-1.308111

international attention to the issue of cyberbullying and the struggles facing LGBT youth.[53]

A tragic loss that should not have happened ... Rest in peace, Ryan.

Ryan (1989–2003), age thirteen, died by suicide after being bullied by students and one other person online. These students were sending him homophobic messages. They also made threats and taunted him all the time.[54]

Here are some raw facts about teen violence:
- One in three teens will be involved in an abusive relationship.[55]
- 33 percent of our youth fall victim to sexual, physical, verbal, or emotional dating abuse.[56]
- Females who are abused by a partner are six times more likely to become pregnant and contract a sexual transmitted disease.[57]
- Dating abuse starts between sixth grade and twelfth grade.

Can you believe that 72 percent of thirteen-and fourteen-years-old are dating? These victims are afraid to report or tell someone because they do not want to reveal themselves, and they truly do not know or understand the laws put into place for domestic and sexual abuse. Speaking of these laws, there are eight states in the United States that do not take into account that violent dating relationships are domestic abuse. So, anyone younger than twenty-five who has been or is being

---

[53] Forderaro, Lisa. "Invasion of Privacy Charges after Death of Tyler Clementi-NYTimes.com," *New York Times* (September 29, 2010): New York: NYTC. ISSN 0362-4331. Retrieved July 7, 2018, from https://www.nytimes.com/2010/09/30/nyregion/30suicide.html

[54] Justin M. Norton, "States Pushing for Laws to Curb Cyberbullying," Fox News, (February 21, 2007): Retrieved July 7, 2018, from https://www.foxnews.com/story/states-pushing-for-laws-to-curb-cyberbullying

[55] Teen Suicide Prevention (2005): Statistics, Facts, Signs, and More – Troubled Teen Help. Retrieved July 7,2018, from http://www.teensuicide.us/articles7.html

[56] Ibid.

[57] Ibid.

abused cannot get a restraining order from the abuser. These states need to change their laws immediately! Sadly, 50 percent of our children who have suffered rape or physical abuse will attempt suicide.[58] Maybe if all states would accept that this abuse is going on and place new laws, we could drastically change that 50 percent who feel suicide is the only answer.

Let's discuss the aftermath of teen dating abuse. As our children start to develop the relationship on an emotional level, it can have positive or negative effects. Of course, a healthy relationship has a positive effect on the children. The unhealthy relationship will cause short-and long-term negative effects on the child who has suffered the abuse. These children will become depressed and have anxiety. This abuse could lead them to drinking or doing drugs. The child could become withdrawn and unsociable. Then, of course, these children may begin to think about killing themselves.

Why do you think our children believe this is acceptable behavior? I will tell you. It is because they learn that violence is normal, and they learn this from adults, peers, and even social media.

When our children learn that violence is normal, the risk of damaging relationships in their future will increase their negative thinking—thinking that violence in a relationship is acceptable and portraying depression, anxiety, and aggression. These children have a higher risk of alcohol and drug use. They become sexually active at a younger age and will also have more sexual partners at the same time. They may associate with other children who have the same thinking patterns, and these children typically experience violence in their home environments.

These types of relationships with our children start early in their lives and will last forever. Unfortunately, these children believe it is normal to tease or call a partner names, but what they do not know is that they are opening the door to become an abuser, which will eventually lead to violence.

---

[58] Teen Suicide Prevention (2005) Statistics, Facts, Signs, and More – Troubled Teen Help. Retrieved July 7,2018, from http://www.teensuicide.us/articles7.html

Teaching our kids to have positive relationships with others is important. Teaching them violence is not acceptable. Parents cannot condone this type of behavior. Let your child know communicating with his or her partner is a key to a healthy relationship.

It's important to teach children how to talk about feelings such as jealousy or what makes them angry. Teach them to respect future partners. Teaching our children will prevent dating violence. This is not a light subject, but it is a very important subject. We must talk to our children about dating and sexual, physical, and mental abuse. We want our children to have a positive experience in the relationships they will endure throughout their lives.

Drug and Alcohol Abuse

Drug and alcohol abuse plays another leading role in suicide. Some parents do not even know their child drinks or does drugs. As I have said, parents need to open their eyes and go ahead and make their children mad. Ask questions, take their phones, look at text messages, find out who their friends are, and then introduce yourself to their friends' parents. Yes, it may piss off your children, but wouldn't you rather piss them off for their safety and your love? You are a parent, not a friend! You must realize that the drugs or alcohol will influence your children more to commit and complete suicide.

What may start out as a fun experiment to the child is something that can lead to an addiction. Being young and impressionable, it is easy for our children to be baited by their peers. Some will decide they do not like the feelings of being high or drunk and will never do it again. Others may love it and become addicts. Sadly, it will cause some to go overboard and overdose. Do they do it on purpose, or is it an accident? The truth is that most just get to a point in their lives when they do it on purpose because they do not want to live like this.

When asking individuals why they turned to drugs or alcohol, their answers can be confusing. They turn to this because they want to hide their emotions, the pain, and the depression. Drugs and alcohol cause a chemical imbalance in the brain. What users do not realize is that their feelings of depression, sadness, and worthlessness intensify from drugs and alcohol. Another problem is the withdrawal symptoms they will go through after a night of partying.

Teen Suicide Prevention expresses on the dependency on drugs and how both legal and illegal substances will lead a child to feel more helpless and more hopeless.[59] Drugs and alcohol will become "necessary" in everyday life. It will become physical and mental to the child, and these feelings will lead the child to feel out of control. Other problems start to take effect when the child is not using drugs or drinking alcohol, including physically being sick and feelings of lowness. These feelings are unpleasant to them and lead to more depression and stronger suicide thoughts and attempts.

There are situations when stress and major life events will contribute to the child's decision to start doing drugs or drinking alcohol. When they experience feelings of being overwhelmed or depressed, the drugs and alcohol seem to make them feel better. This is called self-medicating, which will lead to drug and alcohol abuse and addiction.

Contributing trigger factors of teen depression include stressful events at home and school; exposure to violence and mental, physical, sexual, or emotional abuse; the loss of someone they love; parents who divorce; changes due to financial problems or social situations; and a move to another state or even a different school.

To prevent teen suicide from drug and alcohol abuse, you must know the signs and symptoms of a child who may be involved in drugs and alcohol.

- a new set of friends
- increased secretiveness
- tendency to pull away from family and their normal friends
- no interest in activities and dropping grades
- not caring how they look or even not caring about their hygiene
- funny smells
- bloodshot eyes, a change in coordination, or getting sick

---

[59] Teen Suicide Prevention (2005) Statistics, Facts, Signs, and More – Troubled Teen Help. Retrieved July 7, 2018, from http://www.teensuicide.us/articles7.html

By understanding and recognizing the signs, you are in a better position to save your child from further damage and, most of all, suicide.

Getting the right treatment for your child is crucial to counteract the depression, drug and alcohol abuse, and the suicides that follow this pattern. There are many resources in your community. There are many inpatient and outpatient treatment programs. For more severe children who need help, inpatient treatment programs along with therapy and medications are necessary. Be sure the program includes help with depression and suicide prevention. At this time in your child's life, your thoughts of embarrassment or denial that your child is going through this hard time must be put aside and forgotten. Remember this is not about you and your feelings. It is about your child who needs help. A fact you might have to face is that the problem your child has may be due to you. It is your responsibility to love, care, and be there for your child as long as he or she is living. When supporting a child with an addiction problem, the child must know he or she has your love and support 100 percent.

A tragic loss that should not have happened … Rest in peace, Brodie.

Brodie (1987–2006), age nineteen, was a waitress. She jumped from a high parking garage. Her coworkers were responsible for the bullying. After Brodie took her life, her parents lobbied the Victorian government to amend the Crimes Act 1958 to include serious bullying as a criminal offence. When convicted of this crime, one will face a maximum penalty of ten years.[60]

---

[60] Justine Longmore, "Parliament set to pass brodie's law on bullying," abc. net.au. (May 31, 2011): Archived from the original on August 18, 2017. Retrieved July 7, 2018, from https://www.abc.net.au/news/2011-05-31/ parliament-set-to-pass-brodies-law-on-bullying/2738306

A tragic loss that should not have happened … Rest in peace, Nicola.

Nicola (1985–2001), age fifteen, was a high school student who killed herself by an overdose. She had been bullied for three years because she was gothic. Nicola told her teachers way before she chose suicide. The teachers knew she was being attacked but never informed her parents.[61]

Sexual Orientation

Children who hide their sexual orientation are at a much higher risk for committing suicide. There was a study done of seven thousand students in high school. According to Reuters Health, nearly 4 percent of these students experienced sexual orientation discordance.[62] One of the questions in this study was if the students ever thought about killing themselves, planned on how they would kill themselves, or had ever attempted suicide. Half of the students who had experienced sexual orientation discordance admitted to having suicidal thoughts and behaviors.

Females with nonfatal suicidal thoughts and attempts were found to be more common than students suffering from bullying, those using drugs or alcohol, or those who had been sexually assaulted.

It is said that discrimination, stigma, prejudice, rejection, and societal norms add pressure to these children, forcing them to have a sexual identity problem.[63] It is awful that children feel that their families and friends will turn away if they admit to their true sexual identity. Our LGBT children suffer from depression more than our heterosexual children, making drug abuse, bullying, and violence

---

[61] "Suicide Pupil Was Bullied at School for Three Years; Teacher's Damning Note May Hold the Key as Heartbroken Family Fight for Justice," Mail-on-sunday.vlex.co.uk (October 19, 2005): Archived from the original on July 12, 2012. Retrieved July 7, 2018, from https://infogalactic.com/info/List_of_suicides_which_have_been_attributed_to_bullying

[62] Reuters Health, "Teens Who Hide Their Sexuality Have Higher Suicide Risk, Study Finds," (2018): Retrieved July 3, 2018, from www.huffpost.com

[63] Ibid.

toward the child higher than their heterosexual peers. Most parents know that adolescence is a hard a time for their child, but it is very challenging for LGBT children.

I have more raw facts for you to think about. Healthline Media expressed that 55 percent of LGBT children feel unsafe at school because of their sexual orientation.[64] Our children are being harassed because of their sexual orientation and gender expressions. They are being physically attacked. They are punched or even injured by weapons. Having to deal with a hostile environment affects their mental health. This will affect their grades in school, and they cannot perform academically.

Unfortunately, the abuse they get from their peers does not stop with them. When they go home, they may receive the same reactions from their parents. It is important to know how your reaction to your child's sexual preference will make a huge impact on his or her mental and physical health. There are several parents who do not know how to handle the fact that their child is LGBT. Some parents will go as far as kicking the child out of the home. Other children will simply run away because they cannot deal with the stress from their parents.

LGBT children are also at a higher risk for mental problems than children who are heterosexual.[65] Health risks contribute to violence, unintentional injury, and drug and alcohol abuse, as well as riskier sexual behaviors, depression, bulling, and peer pressure. Lastly, there is a higher risk for suicide and suicide attempts.[66]

Our LGBT children should feel safe at their schools and, most importantly, in their own homes. Our schools can take a stand and start programs and place policies against the harassment of LGBT students. Schools can put together support groups or introduce topics in the classroom about LGBT. Having a supportive school staff can change many problems with our LGBT children.

---

[64] Reuters Health, "Teens Who Hide Their Sexuality Have Higher Suicide Risk, Study Finds," (2018): Retrieved July 3, 2018 from www.huffpost.com

[65] Reuters Health, "Teens Who Hide Their Sexuality Have Higher Suicide Risk, Study Finds," (2018): Retrieved July 3, 2018 from www.huffpost.com

[66] Ibid

Parents, get out of your old ways and learn to communicate with your children. Ask how they are doing at school and at home. It is important to talk, listen, and be very supportive of your child. Learn to be proactive and involved instead of hiding, being angry, or remaining in denial. Again, it is not about your feelings, how others will react, or what you think is wrong or right. It is about your child feeling loved and safe.

A tragic loss that should not have happened … Rest in peace, William.

William (1865–1877), age twelve, was a boarder at Christ's Hospital School in Sussex. He committed suicide by hanging himself. He was being bullied and beaten. Please take another look at the dates. Bullying has been around many years, and it is only getting worse. Something needs to be done about this.[67]

A tragic loss that should not have happened … Rest in peace, Megan.

Megan (1992–2006), age thirteen, committed suicide by hanging herself just three weeks from her birthday. She was a victim of cyberbullying. People would take her information and then later use it to humiliate her.[68]

A tragic loss that should not have happened … Rest in peace, Sladjana.

Sladjana (1992–2008), age sixteen, committed suicide by jumping through a window with a sheet around her neck. She was from another country, and the students were bullying her because of her name and

---

[67] George A. T. Allan, Jack Eric Morpurgo (1984), Christ's Hospital, Town & County, p. 70, ISBN 9780863640056, The immediate cause was the suicide, on 4th May 1877 of a 12 years old Blue. William Gibbs. The outcry that followed forced the Home Secretary to set up a Commission of Inquiry Retrieved July 7, 2018 from https://infogalactic.com/info/List_of_suicides_which_have_been_attributed_to_bullying

[68] "Key events in the Megan Meier case," Associated Press at USA Today (May 15, 2008): Retrieved July 7, 2018, from https://www.smh.com.au/technology/key-events-in-the-megan-meier-case-20080516-2ev8.html

accent. These students taunted her and called her "slutty Jana" and "slut Jana vagina." Sladjana could not deal with any more pain.[69]

Domestic Abuse

It is disturbing to know that many children are not safe in their own homes. My stomach tightens just thinking about all the children who are being abused by the hands and the mouths of their parents. Having three children myself, I could not imagine abusing my children. God did not give me children to abuse them. They are a gift, and those who do not see this truly do not need children.

Children who fall under this category have been beaten and mentally abused. For the children who are suffering, not only is it the abuse they are suffering from but the damage it will cause throughout their lives. They will learn they cannot trust anyone, including themselves. Their self-worth is thrown out the window.

Children may not be victims of abuse themselves but may see it in their homes as witnesses of domestic abuse. This too will have a detrimental effect on them. The parents who are abusers blame the children for their problems and make their children feel ashamed for living. They believe it is their fault and that they are the cause for such havoc in their parents' lives. I cannot for the life of me understand how parents can do this to their own children.

There are some children who can overcome this and grow to become healthy, living adults. Some of the children will grow and become exactly what their parents are and abuse their own children. Then we have the other children who decide that ending their lives is the best way to go. These children commit suicide, believing no good will come from their existence.

This affects me, and I hope it is affecting you. These children need us; they need you. If you know of or see the abuse of children, please

---

[69] Vince Grzegorek, "Family of Sladjana Vidovic, 16-Year-Old Who Committed Suicide, Suing Mentor Schools," *Cleveland Scene*. Retrieved July 7, 2018 from https://www.clevescene.com/scene-and-heard/archives/2010/08/23/family-of-sladjana-vidovic-16-year-old-who-committed-suicide-suing-mentor-schools

report the crime. If you suspect or know that a child is being abused, call the child abuse hotline right away:

800-4-A-CHILD (800-422-4453). If a child is in immediate danger, also call 911. You could be a hero to a child.

Peer Pressure

Our children are surrounded by peer and social stress. When it becomes too much for our children, they end up depressed and suicidal thoughts enter their minds. The Division of Psychiatry at Cincinnati Children's Hospital Medical Center expresses that when a child feels pressured or stressed, he or she will first talk to friends.[70] Therefore, it is so important for everyone to know the signs of depression and suicidal thoughts from a friend in need. Friends and peers need to know when and where to ask for help. Let your children know they can go the friend's parents and tell them what they know. They can also tell a teacher, school counselor, or principal. Be sure your children know that if they do not feel comfortable going to anyone else, they can talk to you and you will act. It is important to share the information to save the friend's life.

Social pressure that can break your child and to make them do the unthinkable could be a number of things, including a breakup, rejection, or crisis at home or school leading to legal problems. Your child may be dealing with humiliation, gossip, teasing, or bullying. And then there's peer pressure and feeling the need to impress everyone. Some struggle with the reality of a pregnancy, overscheduling, having days too full to complete necessary tasks, or feeling pressure to succeed, not to mention social media, school stress, academic stress, and anxiety from taking tests.

If there is no support or maybe the child cannot seem to connect at school, this may lead to a child taking his or her own life. Another

---

[70] Cincinnati Children's Hospital Medical Center (1999–2018). Youth Suicide Prevention-Surviving the Teens® Tips for Parents. Accessed July 7, 2018. https://blog.cincinnatichildrens.org/wp-content/uploads/2016/02/Youth-Suicide-Prevention.pdf

danger to a child is being singled out by a teacher or teachers. This is a red flag for major depression. Are you wondering if this behavior happens in school? The raw fact answer is yes, it is. I have seen this happen to one of my daughters. I am a hands-on mom, and my children will talk to me about anything and come to me if something is going on that makes them angry, sad, or even uncomfortable. Of course, I had a visit with the school and expressed my concerns regarding this matter, and it did stop.

It is completely ridiculous that our children must go through peer pressure and peer harassment and on top of that have to deal with the same childish behavior from a teacher. But it happens. Parents, get involved with your children and let them know you are there for them. If your child is getting in trouble or grades are dropping in one class, then get on top of the problem. There could be an issue with the teacher. I am not here bashing on teachers, but unfortunately, I have been this parent and had to take my daughter out of a class due to the teacher.

It saddens me to report that often suicides are done by perfectionists who were having unbending thinking. Unfortunately, people who fall under the category of perfectionism have a thinking pattern that tells them it is all perfect or all bad. Most of us realize there is no such thing as perfect all the time, and to be honest, that is what pushes people to become better or to keep striving for better. Perfectionist do not think this way; instead, they feel like failures and often come to believe there is no reason to live in a world that isn't perfect. You must think of your child when you add pressure. Pressure can play a positive role, but you must know when too much turns into a negative effect.

A tragic loss that should not have happened ... Rest in peace.

A petite, blonde-haired, blue-eyed high school senior committed suicide after sexting a nude photo to her boyfriend. After they broke up, he sent the photo to the students at her school. She was bullied and taunted with names such as *slut* and *whore*. When she was at school, she would hide in the bathroom to avoid being bullied. She was invited to do an interview on television; she did the interview in hopes that other girls would not fall victim. Two months after her interview she went to a funeral. A boy she knew killed himself. After the funeral, she came home and took her own life. Her mother was the one who found her hanging in her closet.[71]

A tragic loss that should not have happened ... Rest in peace.

A seventh grader committed suicide by hanging herself. She was bullied and teased at school, and later, the cyberbullying started. Her mother would check her daughter's accounts and saw the messages her daughter was receiving from other people. These students were calling her a slut and starting bad rumors at school. Her mother removed her daughter from these apps, so she could not read what the students were saying anymore. The last message she read before hanging herself was that she was stupid and naïve and nobody would miss her. She left a note for her parents expressing she could take any more.[72]

Bullying and Cyberbullying

Bullying is aggressive behavior from school-age children. Bullying has two things: a perceived balance of power and repetition.

According to StopBullying.gov, the bully will access something he or she has—access to embarrassing information, physical power, or popularity—to control or harm others.[73] Bullying happens more than once or has the potential to happen more than once.

---

[71] Emily Bazelon, "Sexting Scourge," *Slate*, (April 10, 2013): Retrieved July 7, 2018, from https://slate.com/human-interest/2013/04/rehtaeh-parsons-rape-case-why-do-these-keep-happening.html

[72] Glenda Luymes, "Cyberbullying: Outpouring of grief over teen's suicide (with video)," *The Province*, (March 25, 2002): Archived from the original on October 14, 2012. Retrieved July 7, 2018, from https://globalnews.ca/news/296421/outpouring-of-grief-over-cyberbullied-b-c-teens-suicide/

[73] "Stop Bullying on the spot" (2018): Retrieved July 7, 2018 from https://www.stopbullying.gov/

Bullying can be emotional, such as one teasing or threatening to cause harm. It can also be social, such as when one threatens to exclude another, or physical, such as when one hits another.

Bullying has severe damaging effects on a child's mental health, leading to feelings of powerlessness as the bully has his or her way over and over. This includes the children who are being bullied, the one doing the bullying, and the children who watch the bullying. The children who have witnessed the bullying have said it makes them feel helpless.

Bullies, victims of bullying, and children who watch the bullying have something in common. They share depression, anxiety, violence, sexual violence, substance abuse, low social functioning, low school performance, and low attendance. Students who bully others and students who fall victim to bullying are at a high risk for suicidal behavior.

As we know today, bullying isn't limited to in-person events. Technology is a wonderful aspect of today's society. We as humans are always looking for a faster way to do things. Our children spend most of their time on their phones and computers. It is easy for children to make friends, find love, and communicate with other children around the world. This technology has its positive aspects, but it also has a downside: cyberbullying is a huge reason why children commit suicide.

Here are some facts about cyberbullying:
- Approximately 43 percent of children have encountered some type of cyberbullying.[74]
- Many children say they are bullied because of their looks, race, or religion.[75]

---

[74] Chris Moessner, "Cyberbullying, Trends and Tudes," NCPC.org. Accessed February 10, 2014, http://www.ncpc.org/resources/files/pdf/bullying/Cyberbullying%20Trends%20-%20Tudes.pdf.

[75] Ibid.

- Children also feel they are easy targets because of their sexuality.[76]
- Nearly 70 percent of children have witnessed cyberbullying.[77]

Our children have an opportunity to go into chat rooms and talk to people they know or make new friends. Some of our children will start to be bullied. Our children are mocked by other users. Our children are being teased by others for the things they like and their beliefs. Some users will make threats or spread rumors, and these rumors can spread quickly over social media. You might be wondering how cyberbullying starts. It can start from one of your child's peers from school. That peer may have a problem with your child and take it upon himself to make stories up about your child. The story becomes a wildfire and spreads all over the world.

Some children can go on with life and delete the ones who are being rude and trying to bully them, but others seem to get stuck and for some reason do not delete these bullies. They continue to read what they are saying. When they allow this to happen, they start to have low self-esteem, from which other problems follow. These children become depressed, and we already know what happens when a child becomes too depressed. In case you forgot, it may lead to suicide. When your child is repeatedly being told how worthless she is or is being told to kill herself because no one cares or loves her, the child eventually gives in to the bullying and kills herself.

A child's phone is the most common place for cyberbullying. Most children will agree that cyberbullying is a growing problem; 81 percent of children agree online bullying is easier for one to get away with his actions than in person.[78] Another fact that blows my mind is that

---

[76] Sandra Graham, "Bullying: A Module for Teachers," Accessed February 10, 2014, http://www.apa.org. http://www.apa.org/education/k12/bullying.aspx#

[77] Ibid.

[78] Ciaran Connolly, "Facts About Cyber Bullying" No Bullying Expert Advice On Cyber Bullying School Bullying. Accessed February 10, 2014, http://nobullying. com/facts-about-cyber-bullying/n

90 percent of children who witness cyberbullying will not report it.[79] There are children who have admitted they have told the bully to stop harassing others. Out of ten victims, only one will tell a parent about the abuse. Girls are being cyberbullied more than boys. Another target that hurts me are the children who are autistic or have Asperger's syndrome. A sad fact is 75 percent of students have admitted to bashing another student online.[80]

Effects of cyberbullying. Our children who suffer from cyberbullying have admitted that bullying had a huge impact on their social lives and damages their self-esteem. Some of our children will turn to self-abuse such as cutting themselves. Also, 30 percent of cyberbully victims have had suicidal thoughts, 10 percent have attempted suicide, and 7 percent will bully others because of their torment.[81]

Parents and teachers need to work together on this problem with the children. Over the years, we have heard a lot about cyberbullying, but the devastating part is research has not proven much progress when it comes to our children and digital aggression.

You may not be able to control what another child will say or do to your child, but you can take control of what is happening. Understand that bullying goes beyond teasing, and no parent has the right to defend it when something is causing this much emotional harm to your child. Parents, be the parent and check your children's computers and phones. See if your child is being bullied or if your child is the one doing the bullying. Remember, it may not seem like a big deal to you, or maybe you feel like you lived through it and are okay. That's not important. Do something if you see your child being bullied or being the bully.

In the next chapter, we'll look at what the teens said in my survey.

A tragic loss that should not have happened ... Rest in peace.

---

[79] Ibid.

[80] Ibid.

[81] "Cyber Bullying: Statistics and Tips," i-SAFE Inc. Accessed February 10, 2014, http://www.isafe.org/outreach/media/media_cyber_bullying

A fourteen-year-old girl committed suicide by hanging herself in her room. Her older sister was the one who found her. Prior to her suicide, students were taunting her and making insults about her weight. She went to a site where one can ask questions and receive help anonymously. She was asking how to help her skin because she had eczema. Unfortunately, there were bullies on this site as well, and the advice she received was to drink bleach and cut herself. Her father found a note written by his daughter after her suicide. Her note read: "As I sit here day by day I wonder if it's going to get better. I want to die; I want to be free. I can't live like this anymore. I'm not happy." Days after her death, her sister who found her started to receive messages mocking the loss of her sister and putting the blame on her father's parenting skills.[82]

A tragic loss that should not have happened … Rest in peace.

A sophomore in high school committed suicide by hanging himself in his backyard because of bullying. His brother said there was no reason for these kids to attack his brother. The boy's older brother posted a statement. I think it is important to share what he talked about. "In today's age, bullies don't push you into lockers, they don't tell their victims to meet them behind the school's dumpster after class. They cower behind usernames and fake profiles from miles away constantly berating and abusing good, innocent people." He went on and expressed that his brother did nothing but have a pretty girlfriend. These bullies broke his spirit.[83]

---

[82] "List of Suicides That Have Been Attributed to Bullying," (2018): Retrieved July 7, 2018, from https://infogalactic.com/info/List_of_suicides_which_have_been_attributed_to_bullying

[83] Ibid.

CHAPTER 5

Interviews with Students

Through my journey on writing about teen suicides, I have interviewed many students. I will not include names to protect them. I will state the age range was from ten to sixteen years of age and grades were from fifth to ninth. I have talked to all types of students. I wanted to show that it does not matter if you are an athlete, a cheerleader, the smartest one in the school, the quiet one, the rich one, or the poor one. There is no age, culture, or color to suicide. All students face depression, anxiety, and too much pressure from school and home. I asked ten basic questions to twenty students (male and female) who came from five different schools. I chose to stop at twenty because all the answers were coming back to be the same. This is proof that our children face many obstacles that we as parents may not have any clue they are facing. The interview included the following questions:

1. Age, grade, and gender
2. Have you witnessed any type of bullying or participated in bullying (laughing, name-calling, etc.)?

3. Do you feel you can talk to your school counselor, teacher, or principal?
4. Are you who you want to be, or are you someone everyone wants you to be?
5. If you could change anything in your school, what would you change?
6. If you could change anything about your school's faculty, what would you change?
7. Does your school talk about bullying and suicide?
8. How safe do you feel at your school?
9. Have you ever felt alone or like no one cares about you?
10. Have you ever thought about suicide?

I will now share the responses from these students, and I am sure you will be as shocked as I was when reading the responses. Remember their names will not be used for their privacy. Children are more prone to talk when they know their names will not be used.

Have you witnessed any type of bullying or participated in bullying (laughing, name-calling, etc.)?

Every student has witnessed bullying. None of the students claimed to participate in any activity. Some of the students did stand up for the one who was being bullied, and others did not involve themselves. From what I have gathered, if a friend was being teased, the student would stand up for the victim, but if the student did not know the victim, then nothing was done about it.

One student responded: "You cannot go a day without getting made fun of. It's a thing now."

Other responses are listed below:
- "Yes, they think it's funny to pick on someone just to make people laugh."

- "Name calling and slapping another student. This student is excluded from most things, and the student can see the individual gets sad."
- "Yes, there was a boy who was being made fun of everywhere he went by everyone for the way he looked and talked. I was going to tell the principle [*sic*], but he stopped showing up at school."
- "Yes, the people who bully do a lot of body shamming."
- "Yes, this kid threw a tennis ball at this other kid's head, but I stood up for this kid."
- "Yes, I see it all the time."
- "Yes, I have witnessed it, and I will help the one who I see being bullied."

I think it is important for families to sit and talk about bullying with their children. Teach them they have to tell an adult or a teacher if they see any type of bullying. If it is your child who is bullying, teach your child this is not okay. Get help for the child, usually there is a reason the child bullies other people. Talk to your children, parents.

A tragic loss that should not have happened … Rest in peace.

A 15-year-old took her life by hanging herself because she fell victim to cyberbullying. She was a new student and was going to a dance with a football player. For this, she was taunted with names such as Irish slut and whore. Following her suicide, these same girls would leave vicious messages on a page created by her family in her memory.[84]

A tragic loss that should not have happened … Rest in peace.

A 13-year-old took his life. He was ridiculed and humiliated by peers at school and online. After his suicide, his father logged in to his account on AOL. His father was looking for clues to why his son killed

---

[84] "List of Suicides That Have Been Attributed to Bullying," (2018): Retrieved July 7, 2018, from https://infogalactic.com/info/List_of_suicides_which_have_been_attributed_to_bullying

himself. To his surprise, some of his son's classmates told him he had been bullied since the fifth grade. His son told a friend something that had happened, and the so-called friend started a rumor about him being gay. After receiving the news, his father now tours around the United States and Canada talking to people and promoting education and prevention of bullying, cyberbullying, and teen suicide.[85]

Do you feel you can talk to your school counselor, teacher, or principal?

From my poll of students, 99 percent indicated they feel they cannot talk to the school counselors, teachers, or the principal. Out of twenty students, only one felt he could reach out to the school's faculty. This number is not acceptable. The following are some of the students' responses:

- "I feel as though they really won't care, and they won't be able to help anyway."
- "I feel like they don't take it seriously and they don't have your best interest in mind."
- "It would make everything worse."
- "They don't care even if you said you were going to kill yourself."
- "Counselors at my school will say random things just to pat you on the back and get you back to class."
- "No, because they mostly do not care."
- "No not really. I have tried to talk to them, but they do not care, and they do nothing anyway."
- "No, because I have misbehaved therefore my relationship with them is not good."
- "Yes, I can but I do not because it does not make the situation better."

Why are our children feeling this way? School faculty is supposed to make our children feel safe and let them know they can come and talk to them. What is happening with our schools? This is another good

---

[85] Ibid

example for parents. You must get involved with your children. This is the only way to make positive steps.

Are you who you want to be, or are you someone everyone wants you to be?

The goal of this question was to test how students were feeling about expressing who they are becoming. Not having self-acceptance can be a part of why people want to kill themselves.

Here are some responses:
- "I am proud of who I am."
- "I am not who I want to be, but I am who I am because of pressure."
- "There are certain people I am myself around, but there are others where I cannot be myself."
- "Yes, I am always me."
- "I am not my true self when at school because I want to be in the main group."
- The following answer comes from a student in fifth grade: "I am not who I exactly want to be because people bother me about when I act like who I really am, so most of the time I try to cover my true self up."
- "I am who I want to be, but still unsatisfied with myself. This is one thing I pride myself on."
- "I only do things if I want to do them, I could care less of what other people think. Life is too short to live for other people and I wish people would realize that tomorrow is not a promise to anyone."

Most of the kids did express they are who they want to be, but the ones who did not seemed to be the younger ones I interviewed. These kids just wanted to be liked by everybody, and this included family. Kids try to make people around them proud at all times. It becomes stressful to them. Parents should let their children know it is okay for them to be themselves and that it is not their responsibility to make everyone happy, especially at the cost of not being themselves.

A tragic loss that should not have happened … Rest in peace.

A 15-year-old whose favorite color was blue took her life on Easter Sunday to end the pain of a cyberbullying. According to her father, the cyberbullying had lasted for months and was carefully documented by the family. As blue was her favorite color, a social media event called blue4grace was started by friends and quickly went viral. When she was in seventh grade, she had met a man online, and he talked her into flashing him her breasts. A year later, the man asked her to 'put on a show' for him. He threatened to release the picture of her breasts to her family and friends if she did not. He knew her address, her name, and the school she went to. The man did release the pictures. Kids at her school saw the pictures and started to bully and tease her. She became severely depressed, developed anxiety, and began to use drugs and alcohol. A year later, she changed schools, and the man came back and created another account using her topless photo as his profile picture. Her new friends started to ignore her, taunt her, and then started bullying her. She began to cut herself. She went to another school to get away from this pain. She changed schools again, which put her back with her first set of bullies. There was a boy who was flirting with her, and because of this, the girls who bullied her from the beginning beat her up while another student was filming the beating. She managed to find her way to the road, where she lay down in a ditch. Her father found her there. Her first attempt was drinking bleach. She continued to cut herself. Her depression and anxiety was getting worse. She attempted suicide again and succeeded. She was live on YouTube when she killed herself. Her parents found her.[86]

---

[86] "List of Suicides That Have Been Attributed to Bullying," (2018): Retrieved July 7, 2018, from https://infogalactic.com/info/List_of_suicides_which_have_been_ attributed_to_bullying

If you could change anything in your school, what would you change?

Although there were a lot of answers that were funny, such as free periods, fewer hours, less homework, and change some rules, there were a few responses that stood out, showing how students feel about where they spend the majority of their day.

- "Add some metal detectors."
- "Make people feel as though they matter."
- "Change the perspective on how one views education because if you get a bad grade you are looked at as if you are dumb."
- "Bad grades should not define your ability of smartness."
- "Change the counselor's, find some who really care."
- "Make the teachers care about the students as much as they care about their paycheck."
- "The amount of kids because there would be less bullies that will cause suicide, and I do not like people."
- "Let kids sell things like cookies or brownies to help with family problems, and let people share food."
- "I would change security making sure no kids have weapons."
- "Have the teachers stop teaching meaningless content and more one-on-one help."
- "Better security, they are old and hate their job so they most likely could not help in a situation."

These stood out to me because these children are afraid and want metal detectors in their schools. They are wanting better security at their schools. These children want their teachers to help more one-on-one. They are asking for their teachers to care for them, not how they appear or what kind of grades they make. A lot of these students complained about their counselors. This is truly heartbreaking.

A tragic loss that should not have happened … Rest in peace.

A thirteen-year-old committed suicide by hanging herself in her bedroom. She sent a nude picture to a boy she liked. A friend of the boy used his phone, saw the picture, and took it upon herself to forward the picture to other students. Insults started, such as slut and whore. School authorities found out about the nude photo toward the end of the school year. The school did act and suspended the girl who forward the picture the first week of eighth grade. When returning back to school after summer, the counselor saw the victim had been cutting herself. The counselor had her sign a no-harm contract. The next day she took her life.[87]

A tragic loss that should not have happened … Rest in peace.

A gay high school freshman took his own life after being bullied by classmates at school and online and receiving death threats by phone. The bullying began with an antigay Facebook group created by classmates. His mother said she knew her son was being harassed and said that her son told her, "Mom, you don't know how it feels to be hated." According to his sister, the abuse that started after he came out was from people he had trusted. "People that were originally his friends, they kind of turned on him. A lot of people, they either joined in or were too scared to say anything."[88]

If you could change anything about your school's faculty, what would you change?

If you are a teacher, you might want to hear what these students had to say about going to school.

---

[87] "List of Suicides That Have Been Attributed to Bullying," (2018): Retrieved July 7, 2018, from https://infogalactic.com/info/List_of_suicides_which_have_been_attributed_to_bullying

[88] Ibid.

- "For teachers to not look so miserable and to try to make the most of their day."
- "Get along with the students."
- "There are too many issues to change."
- "I would let more people like yourself be at the school because you seem to care."
- "I would want them to notice more about what is happening with the students and say something about it when they see wrong doings."
- "I would change the counselors, teachers and basically everything."
- "Give lessons to the teachers on how they should be able to understand and be able to help any student in need."
- "The way counselors and teachers react because they do not do anything to help with kids mentally and they would help only if they changed their reaction."
- "My counselor."
- "Have more than one teacher in class."
- The following answer comes from a fifth grader: "I would change that teachers would not be so mean to students."
- "Also, when a student gets an answer wrong, I would change that teachers would not yell at us."
- "I would want them to explain the answers to us."
- "I would like my teachers to understand me rather than shaming me."
- "The teachers are way better than the elementary and middle school teachers, so I would not change my teachers."

Reading the answers given by the students, it's clear there is a lot of anger and sadness from them. Why is a fifth grader feeling like his teacher makes him feel dumb or is not accepting who he is? I also see children of all ages just want to be respected. Have people become so busy in their lives that the children are being pushed to the side? When asking these students if they talk to their parents, more than half say no because they are too busy, and some said they don't care. I know sometimes kids will feel parents do not care, but it is up to the parents to show they do care about the child, which means the parent has to become involved.

Does your school talk about bullying and suicide?

Responses follow:
- "They are starting too but not really."
- "Not enough, not seriously."
- "Yes, but it does not seem to make a difference."
- "They do not do it enough."
- "Sometimes, but it is short and only once or twice a year."
- "They talk about it a little bit but not enough."
- "No."
- "Only bullying but it does not help."
- "Once in a while."
- "Yes, they have assemblies."
- "They have for bullying but nothing for suicide or a reach out zone for kids who want to die."
- "Not enough."
- "Yes, they have guest speakers come in, but nobody cares about guest speakers."

I know schools are stepping up and doing things such as creating a no-bully zone, and they may have guest speakers come in and talk to the students. Schools have really stepped up over the years, but it is still happening. I believe the statements are strong from schools, but somehow it is not stressed enough. If children do not feel they can talk to their teachers or counselors, then the problem will never end. When it comes to suicide, to me it seems like schools do not want to address it the topic. This topic is huge, and yes, it is scary, but that is why it should be discussed in schools. Let our children know that they can come and talk and get help. Some changes need to be made in schools to let our children feel they do matter and so do their problems.

A tragic loss that should not have happened … Rest in peace.

A seventeen-year-old high school student began receiving threatening emails through her MySpace account. The anonymous emails were of a stalking, terroristic nature. Her parents brought the emails to the attention of the principal of her high school. Because the emails included details of her movements during class and after school, it was obvious that the bully was another student at the school. In October she received an email stating, "I am not going to put you in the hospital, I am going to put you in the morgue." After receiving that email, she did not want to go to school or go out with her friends. Shortly after receiving the threatening email, she took her own life. Her older sister writes: "My little sister committed suicide. I am here to tell you a little about her. She was 17 when she died, and the most amazing girl you would ever meet. She was an out-going, loving, and caring person. You would never dream that she would do that to herself. She was not just my sister; she was my best friend. All I have now is a big, black hole where my heart was. Because my little sister is gone, I won't be able to see her anymore. No more trips to the mall, no more smiles, hugs, late movie nights, nothing. It's gone."[89]

A tragic loss that should not have happened … Rest in peace.

A seventeen-year-old killed himself after being blackmailed into posting pictures of himself online. At his funeral, a parish priest told mourners, "He did not take his own life. His life was taken by these faceless people who put the child into a burning building that he felt he could not escape." A student told his parents about the bullying, and they went to the police, but unfortunately, that did not help.[90]

[89] Jennifer Steinhauer, "Verdict in MySpace Suicide Case," *New York Times*, (November 26, 2008): Retrieved July 7, 2018, from www.nytimes.com/2008/11/27/us/27myspace.html

[90] "List of Suicides That Have Been Attributed to Bullying," (2018): Retrieved July 7, 2018, from https://infogalactic.com/info/List_of_suicides_which_have_been_attributed_to_bullying

This makes me angry! I cannot imagine the pain the parents went through and are still going through. They did what they were supposed to do, but the police let them down. If you are a parent facing this problem, make your voice loud. Take it higher in the police chain. Talk to the news media in your city. Take the child out of the school, but let the school know what is going on with your child. It is heartbreaking when parents reach out for help and try to get protection for their child and our protection does nothing.

How safe do you feel at your school?

The poll on this question seems to be half yes and half no. Here are some responses from students who do not feel safe in their schools:

- "I really do not feel safe because anyone can walk into the school even with the new security they put up."
- "It is stupid because when a student or anyone else pushes the call button they unlock the main door. In trailer buildings anyone can walk into the classroom."
- "I do not always feel safe."
- "I feel a little safe because there is a lot of people, but anyone could bring something dangerous to school and no one would notice."
- "Not very safe."
- "No, literally anyone can shoot up our school."
- "I feel like we have no protection at the school, and harm is waiting."
- "About as safe as I feel anywhere else, which is not very much besides my room. Being safe is just a state of mind for me the only safe place I have is when I am by myself."
- "When I am with my friend, without her not so much."
- "Safe enough."
- "Very safe."
- "Not safe."
- "I feel kind of safe."

- "Not safe at all. I feel like everyone is out to get me."
- "Actually, I hate school there are tons of odd kids walking around with knives and drugs showing them off to friends and threats to kill people on the bus."

Sadly, there have been too many school shootings and the children are afraid to go to school these days. I believe for students who do have fears such as their safety they should be able to talk to a teacher or school counselor about their fears. I also do believe this should not be put into place because there has been a shooting at their school. This should be available for students who have not experienced this type of tragic situation. A child should feel safe at school, and children are asking for better security. I know schools are placing security methods, but maybe it would help if the students knew about the security in their schools. It may allow the children to relax when they are at school.

Have you ever felt alone or like no one cares about you?

Some students really feel alone. Their responses follow:
- "Yes, all the time like no one can hear me."
- Two students said the following: "Yes, when my parents went through a divorce."
- The following answer came from an eleven-year-old: "Sometimes I feel alone, and no one cares when I try my best, but I don't succeed."
- "Yes, when I was in sixth grade, I am now in eighth grade."
- "Yes, all the time but I know my whole family especially my mom is there for me, but I would rather not be around than talk about my problems."
- "Yes, but I know I have tons of people who care for me, but at times they are not there in my mind and this is when thoughts are deadly and it can eat you at you."

- "A big part of that is how much trust a person has."
- "When you have trust issues it is hard to tell who is the closest to you and sometimes you do not even know yourself and you think you are okay, but it is a cover-up and masks the sadness."

Out of twenty students, only four said they did not feel alone or feels like no one cares. There is a problem with this number. I cannot express enough how important it is to sit and listen to your children, creating a safe place for them to bring their problems. You don't have to solve every little thing they bring to you at that point. But listening goes a long way to letting them feel like they have a place to turn when they are overwhelmed.

Have you ever thought about suicide?

Only six students out of twenty said they have never thought about suicide.

The following answers are heartbreaking:
- "Yes, almost every day, but gradually it gets better somedays."
- "Yes, a long time ago."
- "No, but I have cried just thinking why."
- "Yes, the first time I broke-up with my boyfriend."
- The following response is from a fifth grader: "Yes, because I was bullied and felt alone because the school does not do anything, and the counselor did not even care how I felt so I had no one so I was sad and felt like I did not belong at school or anywhere."
- "Yes, when my friends bullied me in first grade."
- "Yes in sixth grade."
- "Yes, mostly caused by school. It causes too much stress and leads to bad thoughts shutting everyone out."
- "Not personally but suicide itself and how a person gets there I can understand."
- "When you are a young person it is very easy to get to a severely dark place and have such thoughts about suicide."

When reading these replies, it hit me to the core. Even if one child said he had thought about killing himself, the number is too high. I am sure a lot of us at one time or another in our lives may have thought about suicide, but for some reason, these kids are actually following through with their thoughts. Help is needed everywhere for our children.

A tragic loss that should not have happened ... Rest in peace.

> Sorry I am a disappointment ...
> Wish I could rewind ...
> I am sorry ...
> Dad
> 13 years of age[91]

A tragic loss that should not have happened ... Rest in peace.

> Sorry to the ones who cared ...
> To my haters ...
> You got your wish ...
> 14 years of age[92]

A tragic loss that should not have happened ... Rest in peace.

> I am sorry for being a burden to you ...
> You are better off without me ...
> I cannot take my meaningless life anymore ...
> 12 years of age[93]

I spoke with many children of all ages, and they were all saying the same things. They had the same responses. This is not just a local problem. This is happening everywhere, in every state, and in every

---

[91] Bing, "Sad Suicide Notes," (2018): Retrieved July 7, 2018, from http:///bing.com
[92] Ibid
[93] Ibid.

country. When looking at the statistics that were stated earlier, it is just mind-blowing. Be inspired to be their voice—the voice they cannot find, the voice that will save them, the voice that will protect them, the voice they will hear saying, "I love you," "You are not alone," and, "You are wanted."

Our children are killing themselves. What is happening to our youth? Why is it that the only answer they have is to kill themselves? Where did we fall short with our children? Why do our children feel as if they have no one they can trust, that no one loves them, that no one will miss them, or that their existence does not matter?

It is time to stand up and be parents to our children and to other children. They need us. They need to know that life offers good, and it is not always going to be this hard. We need to love them, care for them, and get in their business. You need to sit back and watch your child, learn your child, look for signs, and listen for signs.

Have you noticed I have stated "your child" and "our children" throughout this book? As parents and adults, we have a job, and that job is to make sure all children are safe, even if they do not live in our homes. These children have no clue how to raise themselves or deal with adult problems, and surely, they are not equipped to make such a big decision about suicide.

I know we have all suffered from some type of depression, anxiety, or feelings of being alone and have wondered why life sucks at times. I know we have all suffered from a broken heart or two, and I know we have all lost loved ones. I share these feelings with my children. It is important that we teach them that life does suck sometimes, but it turns around and we find a way to move on from our hurting stage. Yes, I also tell them there will be a lot of bumps in life. And then I follow up by telling them we can get past them and live a happy life even with the hard times.

A tragic loss that should not have happened … Rest in peace.

> I love you …
> You cannot cut my hair …
> I love my hair …
> You don't love me enough …
> 12 years of age to a mom and dad[94]

A tragic loss that should not have happened … Rest in peace.

> I am done …
> The world is cruel and twisted …
> This is my escape …
> 16 years of age[95]

---

[94] Bing (2018) Sad Suicide Notes. Retrieved July 7, 2018 from http:///bing.com

[95] Ibid

CHAPTER 6

What a Parent Must Do

As I sit here and wonder how many parents are asking if I have ever had to handle a suicide situation in my family, my answer is yes. My child came to me in fourth grade and asked me how she could meet her maker. My heart sank, and the pain was awful. I will never forget that moment. The reason why she wanted to meet her maker was due to the bullying at school. I was very active, and I took the problem to the board. Not too long after, the bullying stopped. It stopped with my child, but unfortunately, it did not stop for the other children.

A few months ago, my stepdaughter tried to take her life by jumping off a bridge. She did not die, but she had to have major surgery on her foot and ankle. She suffers from addiction. She and I are close and always have been. Her mother was not in her life until a much later age. Unfortunately, her mother is an addict, and they started doing drugs together. I stood by my daughter, but she wanted her biological mother's love.

The night she jumped off the bridge she was with her mom getting high, and she told me this, "Mom, I jumped because I cannot take this way of life anymore. I wanted to see if my mom would stop me, but she didn't. She watched and then left me there screaming in pain."

Every child needs somebody, even if that child is not yours biologically. If you are human, you would will never turn your back on a child crying out for help.

I have always stayed on top of my children and my children's friends. Being a counselor, I have had the privilege speaking to many of their friends. I say privilege because they trust me, and they are comfortable talking to me.

They know they can come to me, and our conversations are confidential. You do not need a degree in counseling to be there for others, to give support to them, and to seek the help they truly need. Again, it is time to stand up and fight for the children who feel they have no one in their lives. We can help and change the numbers—the numbers of children taking their lives.

When I was in my twenties, I wrote a poem, which was published, and I never would have thought I would write a book and put my poem in the book. I am sharing my poem because I think it is important for our children to know that as adults we suffer too, and we have truly walked in their shoes.

Just a Message

It seems at this point in life I don't know where I
  belong.
What I have found out are the disappointments we
  all face in our life.
In the disappointments we will feel angry and hurt,
And it is okay to feel both.
What we must have is our faith and strength.
Remember, when there is bad, good will always
  follow.
We don't know when,
But it's our faith and strength that will keep us
  intact.
I learned that it's not enough to believe in God,
Because the devil himself believes in God.

So, in that, even the bad has faith,
He just doesn't have the strength to keep himself
    intact.
Have faith and be strong,
God would never face us with a disappointment we
    couldn't handle;
He has faith in the strength he gave us.

The following suggestions can help you know what to do if you encounter a child contemplating suicide.

Take it seriously. If your child says, "I want to kill myself," or, "I'm going to commit suicide," always take the statement seriously and immediately seek assistance from a qualified mental health professional. Your child may tell you it was a joke, but this is not a joke. Children mean what they say.

A tragic loss that should not have happened … Rest in peace, Rehtaeh.

Rehtaeh (1995–2013), age seventeen, was a high school student who attempted suicide by hanging, which led to a coma. Later, her life support was turned off. Rehtaeh took her life because four boys ganged raped her. After the boys raped her, they posted pictures online, and she was bullied and harassed. The justice system failed her, and her decision led her to death.[96]

A tragic loss that should not have happened … Rest in peace.

    You never notice …
    Don't stand at my grave …
    Crying and noticing now …

---

[96] "Rehtaeh Parsons Video Tribute Marks Life Of 'Angel' (VIDEO)," *Huffington Post Canada* (April 9, 2013): Retrieved July 7, 2018, from https://ipfs.io/ipfs/ QmXoypizjW3WknFiJnKLwHCnL72vedxjQkDDP1mXWo6uco/wiki/Suicide_ of_Rehtaeh_Parsons.html

15 years of age[97]

A tragic loss that should not have happened … Rest in peace.

> Finding me …
> Receiving a call …
> School announcement …
> Your teasing and bullying …
> You were cruel …
> I gave my life up …
> Bye …
> 14 years of age[98]

Watch them. Find out if the teen has suicidal thoughts, a plan for the suicide, and the means to attempt the suicide. The more specific the plan, the higher the degree of risk for the teenager. If you would notice your child giving things away to friends or even another family member, this is considered a red flag. If you hear your child say things such as, "I wish I was dead," "I should just kill myself," "Nobody likes me," or "Nobody would notice if I was gone," these are all red flags. Some children may even have a goodbye letter written. Whatever it may be or whatever you find or hear, take it seriously and seek help.

Remove dangers. Tell the child that you will do whatever you can to prevent him from committing suicide. Remove or securely lock guns, pills, medications, and other potential lethal means and make them out of reach of the child.

Other popular methods are asphyxiation, cutting, overdosing, and carbon monoxide poisoning. Family and friends of someone with high-risk suicidal behavior must take the steps and put away knives, pipes, rope, and medication.

You must take suicidal threats seriously. It does not matter if you think this child has a good life. You do not know what may be going

---

[97] Bing, "Sad Suicide Notes," (2018): Retrieved July 7, 2018, from http:///bing.com
[98] Ibid

on inside this child. You must take the suicidal thought and or threat seriously, treat it as an emergency, and take the child and act at once.

Following these steps could be life changing to the child and yourself. One should never think twice when a child is contemplating suicide. One should never yell or make remarks to a child wanting to kill herself. It could be your last response that pushes the child to follow through with the suicide.

Children who are planning to commit suicide must seek help immediately from a friend, family member, health care provider, or mental health professional. If a child tells you directly, call a mental health care professional immediately. There are a lot of resources that one can find and that are available 24/7. Family members, friends, teachers, and your community can provide you with comfort and moral support.

Having healthy relationships. The Office of Suicide Prevention stresses how parents can help prevent a child from committing suicide. You must have a good relationship with your child. In early childhood development, your child bonds with you and learns to have trust in you. This allows the child to trust the outside world and teaches him to grow and develop in different stages throughout life. When children enter the adolescent years, they are pushed to come to terms with fast physical growth, conflicts with you and friends, and emotional and physical intimacy. They are trying to figure out what they want to do when they grow up.

It may seem your child does not want to have a close relationship with you or maybe no relationship at all, but to be honest, your child is starving for that parent-child relationship. We must grow with our children. This is a two-way street, parents. When having a strong and loving relationship with our children, they, in return, will have respect for our values. They will also ask for our advice and our support in stressful times.

Having a strong relationship with your child opens the door of good communication, and this is lifesaving to your depressed and troubled child. Communication will lead parents to support the child and intervene before your child commits suicide.

Part of these relationships includes ensuring there is a stable, safe home life. Although this sounds obvious, there are many children living on the streets because of this problem. Divorce can also be extremely stressful for children, and it's important that both partners support the children as they separate.

Spending a great deal of time with your child doing fun family activities will help your child reflect on the positive times when he or she is upset with you. You do not want the time spent with your child to always be a negative experience. You will have arguments with your child, and both of you will be upset. But when alone and cooling off, good memories come along, and it takes off the edge from the argument.

Listen to your child. You must learn to not speak too much while your child is telling you about his or her feelings. A lot of children complain about their parents and how they do not understand them because they do not listen to them. Parents often do not take the time to truly listen to their children's points of view. Their feelings and points of view are important to them, so listen fully.

You must learn the line between being supportive and being intrusive. Parents need to know how to acknowledge their children when they are upset. If your child comes home and it is obvious that he had a bad day, just go to him, hug him, and tell him you love him. If he needs to talk, you are there waiting to listen. Do not interrogate or demand that your children tell you their problems or secrets. If you have a good relationship with your children, they will talk to you about their situations when they are comfortable and ready. Remember that it is possible for your children to solve their problems without talking to you all the time. Be supportive when they ask or reach out.

Our children will hide or explode their emotions, so it is important for us to encourage our children to express their happy moments and sad moments. When teaching our children to express feelings such as happiness or excitement from something they accomplished, it helps them to express moments of disappointment and sadness. This will help your children not to hide all their feelings even if they are bad, which helps them to not be explosive.

In the next chapter, we'll look at more things parents can do after a suicide attempt.

CHAPTER 7

After a Suicide Attempt

Intervention after your child has attempted suicide can be hard. We cannot be afraid to approach our children because we fear they will try suicide again.

If your child is on medication, research the medications to determine if there is a risk for suicide. Disorders such as bipolar, schizophrenia, and anorexia nervosa often present in teen years. There are medications to help these conditions, but medications can induce psychosis. In other words, the medications can help with the disorder, but they also put our children at a higher risk of suicide. It is important that children are managed carefully with their doctor while on medication.

If your child is prescribed these types of medicines, there are certain symptoms you should look closely for.

- depression, agitation, or the beginning of panic attacks
- hallucinations, such as hearing voices or seeing things
- onset of delusions, meaning having a false belief about something
- mood swings from high to low
- extreme ideas that affect the child's day-to-day functions

If you should notice any of these signs or symptoms, they may be due to an underlying psychiatric illness from the medication your child was prescribed. Take your child back to the doctor where they can be assessed by a professional.

The first step after a suicide is ensuring that you are working with a doctor to help uncover the reasons for the suicide attempt and to help your child with what she is struggling with. After that, the following can be helpful:

- Make sure your child is safe by removing dangerous weapons.
- Always be available but do not be overly protective.
- Keep your eyes open. Observe your child, but do it discreetly. It is important that your child returns to his regular schedule prior to the suicide attempt.
- Do not make your child talk about the suicide attempt. Only talk about the attempt when your child approaches you. You do not want to push or upset the child if he is not ready to talk about what happened.
- Keep reaching out to support groups and prevention hotlines. Learn what you don't know, and take action to help your family.

It is important to understand that all suicides be taken with action. Meaning, if you see changes in a child or you hear statements about wanting killing herself, act and get help. You cannot think the child is just saying this for attention no matter how many times you hear it. It is your job to act and seek help every time. What you do not want to do is dismiss what your child just went through. Your child did not do this for attention! Without the proper help, your child will try again.

Parents, you are not forgotten or overlooked during a time like this. I know parents, other family members, and friends go through emotions such as sadness, anger, and confusion. There are several places to go for help for parents and all who are involved in your child's life. Your family doctor can give you resources, and you can look online for support groups in your area, as well as suicide hotlines. Suicide affects everyone who is around the child, and it is just as important for you to seek help. You cannot do this alone.

A tragic loss that should not have happened ... Rest in peace.

> No one asked ...
> I was not okay ...
> This is selfish ...
> You are more selfish ...
> Too late to notice now ...
> 15 years of age[99]

A tragic loss that should not have happened ... Rest in peace.

> Manic depression ...
> Burdens on my chest ...
> I want to die ...
> I am tired of lying ...
> Making my mom cry ...
> 13 years of age[100]

---

[99] Bing, "Sad Suicide Notes," (2018): Retrieved July 7, 2018, from http:///bing.com
[100] Ibid.

CHAPTER 8

Conclusion

One of the best preventions for suicide is when the child knows he or she has support during tough times. This is something you can begin to build right now—today—with your children or the children in your circle.

Start talking to them. Employ active listening skills to show you understand. Give them your time in the big things and the little things. It is a fact that if a child has an important person or role model, it can decrease the child's thoughts of suicide. This is important for those children who may not have a good home environment. When someone reaches out and becomes a permanent positive fixture, the child will have more of a reason to live. That child will strive to rise above his or her problems. You can think of this person being the child's lifeline.

If your child has good coping skills, he or she is more than likely to use these skills and will be able to cope with the stressors in life. Typically, if a child knows how to apply coping skills, that child may just see a difficult situation as a challenge, giving him or her the opportunity to change the situation and rise above.

Having a supportive and caring family is a powerful tool to our children. When we come together as a unit, the whole family will benefit, especially our children. Our children need love, care, and, most importantly, understanding. Our children also need guidance, communication, stability, and rules.

Putting your child in activities such as sports, church groups, or any type of scouts is also a great idea. When staying active, the child can use energy by being involved instead of constantly thinking about the negatives in life. This is also a learning tool. That child will learn how to relate to others, which will raise the child's self-esteem.

These areas are important in your child's life. Act and implement these areas into your lives and into your family's lives. As a result, you could be one of the parents who saves a child's life.

Throughout this book, I have shared the stories of children who committed suicide and their last words, hoping they affect your next decision. This goes for the children who want to end their lives, parents, peers, and teachers. Reading these stories made me cry, made me sad, and mad me angry. I just wish someone could have changed their minds before they ended their lives. I hope the children who were involved with these children's suicides were forced to take responsibility for their part. My heart goes out to their families and friends who were affected by each of these suicides. People are so mean and cruel.

Do not fall victim. Ask for help. It's not too late to change your environment and find good in this life. You may not feel loved at this time, but *you are loved by many. I promise you that!*

Suicide is real, and it is happening everywhere. It does not matter who you are; it is the devil playing in your playground, and you must be strong and beat him at his own game. No one is alone. Seek help and help others. Remember, situations will change, but suicide is forever.

If you're feeling suicidal, please tell someone. There is help for dealing with the overwhelming feelings you have. If you know someone who is, don't be afraid to approach these children to express your concern. Religious groups and community organizations are also a valuable resource. In addition, there are many suicide hotlines that provide anonymous assistance. One of them is the National Suicide Prevention Lifeline at 800-273-TALK (8255) or contact the Crisis Text Line by texting TALK to 741741.

Please share this book with parents, peers, teachers, and children who you think might need help. *Let's start saving lives together!*

RESOURCES

Recommended for Further Information

Books for Families, Teens, Peers, and Teachers

A Relentless Hope: Surviving the Storm of Teen Depression by Gary Nelson (2007) 9781556353093

> Nelson offers compassionate, practical help for exploring questions and concerns related to teen depression. The book "is written for teens, parents, teachers, pastors, and who walk with the afflicted through this valley of the shadow of death."

Aftershock: Help, Hope, and Healing in the Wake of Suicide by David Cox and Candy Arrington (2003) 9780805426229

> Most people do not know how to react to or comfort families after a suicide. This book can help with grief and healing.

Is Your Teen Stressed or Depressed? by Dr. Arch Hart and Dr. Catherine Hart Weber (2008) 9780785289401

> "A practical and inspirational guide for parents of hurting teenagers."

My Friend Is Struggling with Thoughts of Suicide by Josh McDowell and Ed Stewart (2008) 9781845503574

> These two writers offer "biblical insight and practical instruction on what your friends can do when plagued with thoughts of ending it all. But more importantly, you will discover how to become a true source of help and encouragement to lift them from discouragement and despair. And if you are that person struggling with despair, you can learn how to find that light at the end of a dark tunnel you seem to be in."

No More Bullies: For Those Who Wound or Are Wounded by Frank Peretti (2003) 9780849943362

> Peretti describes the emotional pain and physical abuse he endured at the hands of his classmates and offers encouragement to those who have been hurt. He also counsels those who have wounded others and gives advice to parents and teachers about preventing bullying.

The Reason by Lacy Sturm (2014) 9780801016738

> "With raw vulnerability, a rock princess tells her story of physical abuse, depression, and suicidal struggles. She shows beyond the temporary highs and soul-crushing lows is a reason each of us exists and purpose for our lives.

> *Too Soon to Say Goodbye: Healing and Hope for Victims and Survivors of Suicide* by Susan Titus Osborn, Karen Kosman, and Jeenie Gordon (2010) 9781596692435

Online Resources

Accredited Schools Online: Bullying Awareness Guidebook www.mscasa.org/accredited-schools-online-releases-the-bullying-awareness-guidebook/

This guidebook offers information on the cycle of bullying and how to catch it. Another section details the different kinds of cyberbullying and physical bullying, as well as signs to look for. It also has a section dedicated to bullying prevention and how to help.

Means Matter
    https://www.sprc.org/resources-programs/means-matter-website
    The Means Matter website promotes activities intended to reduce a suicidal person's access to lethal means of suicide.

Preventing Suicide: A Tool-Kit for High Schools
    https://youth.gov/feature-article/preventing-suicide-toolkit-high-schools
    Assists high schools and school districts in designing and implementing strategies to prevent suicide and promote behavioral health. Includes tools to implement a multifaceted suicide prevention program that responds to the needs and cultures of students.

ReachOut
    https://schools.au.reachout.com/articles/suicide
    The ReachOut.com website helps teens and young adults facing tough times and struggling with mental health issues. All content is written by teens and young adults, for teens and young adults.

Safe and Effective Messaging for Suicide Prevention
    www.sprc.org/keys-success/safe-messaging-reporting
    This document offers evidence-based recommendations for creating safe and effective messages to raise public awareness that suicide is a serious and preventable public health problem.

Society for the Prevention of Teen Suicide
    https://www.sprc.org/resources-programs/society-prevention-teen-suicide-spts

The Society for the Prevention of Teen Suicide promotes public awareness of teen suicide through educational training programs for teens, parents, and educators.

Suicide Prevention Resource Center: Online Library
https://www.edc.org/suicide-prevention-resource-center-resource-library
The Suicide Prevention Resource Center's online library has many topics with resources.

Suicide Prevention Resources for Parents/Guardians/Families
http://www.sprc.org/resources-programs/suicide-prevention-resources-parentsguardiansfamiliesA list of websites and other online information that have prevention resources for parents, guardians, and other family members.

Suicide Prevention Resources for Teens and Teachers

A list of websites with suicide prevention resources for teens, including those who may be at risk for suicide and those who have friends who may be at risk.

The Role of High School Mental Health Providers in Preventing Suicide
http://www.sprc.org/resources-programs/role-high-school-mental-health-providers-preventing-suicide-sprc-customized
This information sheet is for mental health staff that the school has designated as being responsible for handling student mental health crises.

The Role of High School Teachers in Preventing Suicide
http://www.sprc.org/resources-programs/role-high-school-teachers-preventing-suicide-sprc-customized-information-page
An information sheet that helps teachers understand why suicide prevention fits the role of teacher.

National Center for the Prevention of Youth Suicide/ American Association of Suicidology Resources

Fact Sheet about Youth Suicidal Behavior

A fact sheet about youth suicidal behavior based on 2010 statistics. Fact sheet about suicidal behavior among lesbian, gay, bisexual, and transgender youth. A fact sheet about suicidal behavior among the LGBT community.

AAS School Suicide Prevention Specialist Accreditation

For school psychologists, social workers, counselors, nurses, and all others dedicated to or responsible for reducing the incidents of suicide and suicidal behaviors among today's school-age youth.

BIBLIOGRAPHY

"3 U.S. teens arrested for sexual battery after girl's suicide." CBC News. (April 12, 2013): Accessed July 7, 2018. https://www.cbc.ca/news/world/3-u-s-teens-arrested-for-sexual-battery-after-girl-s-suicide-1.1312171

"A Father Fights Bullying." (May 14, 2010): Accessed July 7, 2018. https://www.greatschools.org/gk/articles/a-father-fights-bullying/

"Amanda Todd Tribute Honors Life of Bullied Teen." News. Calgary, CA: CBC. (November 18, 2012): Accessed July 7, 2018. https://www.cbc.ca/news/canada/british-columbia/amanda-todd-tribute-honours-life-of-bullied-teen-1.1138838

Associated Press. "Jadin Bell Dead: Gay Oregon Teen Who Hanged Himself Dies After Being Taken Off Life Support." *Huffington Post* (February 4, 2013): Accessed July 7, 2018. https://www.huffpost.com/entry/jadin-bell-dead-gay-oregon-teen-hanging_n_2617909.

Bazelon, Emily. "Sexting Scourge." *Slate* (April 10, 2013): Accessed July 7, 2018. https://slate.com/human-interest/2013/04/rehtaeh-parsons-rape-case-why-do-these-keep-happening.html.

"B.C. Girl Convicted in School Bullying Tragedy." CBC News (March 26, 2002): Accessed July 7, 2018. https://www.cbc.ca/news/canada/b-c-girl-convicted-in-school-bullying-tragedy-1.308111.

Bing. "Sad Suicide Notes." (2018): Accessed July 7, 2018. http://bing.com.

Boseley, Sarah. "Suicide Kills One Person Worldwide Every 40 Seconds, WHO Report Finds."

(September 4, 2014): Accessed July 7, 2018. https://www.theguardian.
com/society/2014/sep/04/suicide-kills-every-40-seconds-who

"Bullied 13-year-old said teachers "didn't do anything" in his suicide
note" (2016): Accessed July 7, 2018. https://ph.theasianparent.com/
teachers-didnt-do-anything

"Bullied to Death: Taunted London Teen Commits Suicide." Associated
Press (October 1998): Accessed July 7, 2018. http://www.bibble.org/
misc/bullied_to_death.html.

Casting Crowns. *Just Be Held.* Universal Music Publishing Group,
ESSENTIAL MUSIC PUBLISHING, CAPITOL CHRISTIAN
MUSIC GROUP, Kobalt Music Publishing Ltd. Released 2018.

Cincinnati Children's Hospital Medical Center (1999–2018). Youth
Suicide Prevention-Surviving the Teens® Tips for Parents. Accessed
July 7, 2018. https://blog.cincinnatichildrens.org/wp-content/
uploads/2016/02/Youth-Suicide-Prevention.pdf

Connolly, Ciaran. "Facts About Cyber Bullying." No Bullying Expert
Advice on Cyber Bullying School Bullying. Accessed February 10,
2014. https://www.stopbullying.gov/media/facts/index.html

"Cyber Bullying: Statistics and Tips." i-SAFE Inc. Accessed February
10, 2014. https://auth.isafe.org/outreach/media/media_cyber_
bullying

Dubreuil, Jim and Eamon McNiff. "Bullied to Death in America's
Schools-ABC News." Accessed July 7, 2018. https://abcnews.
go.com/2020/TheLaw/school-bullying-epidemic-turning-deadly/
story?id=11880841.

Forderaro, Lisa. "Invasion of Privacy Charges after Death of Tyler
Clementi-NYTimes.com." *New York Times* (September 29, 2010):
New York: NYTC. ISSN 0362-4331. Accessed July 7, 2018. https://
www.nytimes.com/2010/09/30/nyregion/30suicide.html.

George A. T. Allan, Jack Eric Morpurgo (1984), Christ's Hospital, *Town
& County*, p. 70, ISBN 9780863640056, The immediate cause was
the suicide, on 4th May 1877 of a 12 years old Blue. William Gibbs.
The outcry that followed forced the Home Secretary to set up a
Commission of Inquiry Accessed July 7, 2018.

"Grand Jury Indicts 9 Students in Connection with Phoebe Prince Bullying Case." Gazettenet.com. Accessed July 7, 2018. www.cnn.com/2010/CRIME/03/29/massachusetts.bullying.suicide/index.html

Graham, Sandra. "Bullying: A Module for Teachers." Accessed February 10, 2014. http://www.apa.org. http://www.apa.org/education/k12/bullying.aspx#.

Grzegorek, Vince. "Family of Sladjana Vidovic, 16-Year-Old Who Committed Suicide, Suing Mentor Schools." *Cleveland Scene*. Accessed July 7, 2018. https://www.clevescene.com/scene-and-heard/archives/2010/08/23/family-of-sladjana-vidovic-16-year-old-who-committed-suicide-suing-mentor-schools.

Howlett, Karen. "Anti-bullying Bill Passes, Clearing Way for Gay-Straight Alliances in Ontario Schools." *The Globe and Mail* (June 5, 2012): Accessed July 7, 2018. https://www.theglobeandmail.com/news/politics/anti-bullying-bill-passes-clearing-way-for-gay-straight-alliances-in-ontario-schools/article4231542/.

"Kenneth Weishuhn, Gay Iowa Teen, Commits Suicide after Allegedly Receiving Death Threats." *Huffington Post* (April 17, 2012): Accessed July 7, 2018. https://www.huffpost.com/entry/kenneth-weishuhn-gay-iowa-teen-suicide_n_1431442.

"Key events in the Megan Meier case." Associated Press at *USA Today* (May 15, 2008): Accessed July 7, 2018. https://www.smh.com.au/technology/key-events-in-the-megan-meier-case-20080516-2ev8.html.

"List of Suicides That Have Been Attributed to Bullying." (2018): Accessed July 7, 2018. https://infogalactic.com/info/List_of_suicides_which_have_been_attributed_to_bullying.

Longmore, Justine. "Parliament Set to Pass Brodie's Law on Bullying." abc.net.au. Archived from the original on August 18, 2017. Accessed July 7, 2018. https://www.abc.net.au/news/2011-05-31/parliament-set-to-pass-brodies-law-on-bullying/2738306.

Luymes, Glenda. "Cyberbullying: Outpouring of Grief over Teen's Suicide (with video)." *The Province* (March 25, 2002): Archived from

the original on October 14, 2012. Accessed July 7, 2018. https://
globalnews.ca/news/296421/outpouring-of-grief-over-cyberbullied-
b-c-teens-suicide/ Moessner, Chris. "Cyberbullying, Trends and
Tudes." NCPC.org. Accessed February 10, 2014, file:///C:/Users/
Tracey/AppData/Local/Packages/Microsoft.MicrosoftEdge_
8wekyb3d8bbwe/TempState/Downloads/Trends%20&%20
Tudes%20-%20Harris%20Interactive%20(1).pdf

Nemours Foundation. "Why Do Teens Try to Kill Themselves?"
Accessed July 5, 2018. https://kidshealth.org.

Norton, Justin M. "States Pushing for Laws to Curb Cyberbullying."
Fox News (February 21, 2007): Accessed July 7, 2018. https://www.
foxnews.com/story/states-pushing-for-laws-to-curb-cyberbullying.

Office of Suicide Prevention. "The Myths & Facts of Youth Suicide."
(2019): Accessed July 7, 2018. suicideprevention.NV.gov/Youth/
Myths/.

"Preventing Intimate Partner Violence." Centers for Disease Control
and Prevention. Accessed July 7, 2018. https://www.cdc.gov/
violenceprevention/intimatepartnerviolence/fastfact.html.

"Rebecca Sedwick Case: Bullied Girl and Her Tormentor Both Grew
Up in 'disturbing' family situations, says sheriff." Accessed July
7, 2018. https://www.nydailynews.com/news/national/rebecca-
sedwick-case-suicide-victim-bully-grew-disturbing-family-homes-
article-1.1496991.

"Rehtaeh Parsons Video Tribute Marks Life Of 'Angel' (VIDEO)."
Huffington Post Canada (April 9, 2013): Accessed July 7, 2018.
https://ipfs.io/ipfs/QmXoypizjW3WknFiJnKLwHCnL72vedx
jQkDDP1mXWo6uco/wiki/Suicide_of_Rehtaeh_Parsons.html.

Reuters Health. "Teens Who Hide Their Sexuality Have Higher
Suicide Risk, Study Finds." (2018): Accessed July 3, 2018.
https://www.huffpost.com/entry/lgbtq-teen-suicide-study_n_
5ab264a9e4b008c9e5f33951

Robinson-Buffalo. M. "Sexually Assaulted Teens at Greater Risk of
Suicide." *Futurity*. Accessed. April 6, 2015 https://www.futurity.
org/sexually-assault-boys-suicide-891742/.

"School teasing blamed in Surrey teen's suicide" Archived from the original on May 12, 2001. Accessed July 7, 2018. https://www.cbc.ca/news/canada/school-teasing-blamed-in-surrey-teen-s-suicide-1.221495.

Steinhauer, Jennifer. "Verdict in MySpace Suicide Case." *New York Times* (November 26, 2008): Accessed July 7, 2018. www.nytimes.com/2008/11/27/us/27myspace.html.

Teen Help.com. "Emotional Abuse." (2018): Accessed July 1, 2018. https://www.teenhelp.com.

Teen Suicide Prevention. "Statistics, Facts, Signs, and More – Troubled Teen Help." (2005): Accessed July 7,2018. http://www.teensuicide.us/articles7.html.

Teen Suicide Statistics. "Teen Suicide Facts." (2018): Accessed July 7, 2018. http://teensuicidestatistics.com/statistics-facts.html.

Printed in the United States
By Bookmasters